The Knowledge of London

One Man's Journey

By Andy Cabman

CONTENTS

Army Memoirs

Contents

Introduction

Why be a black cab driver and put yourself through so much pain studying the Knowledge? There are many benefits of being a London black cab driver. The first one is being your own boss and having true freedom. With a lot of self employed jobs, a tradesman for example you may be your own boss but you need to price jobs, quote jobs, organize everything and that's before you even start work, then after you have done the work you have invoices to prepare then you may have to wait for your money to be paid. If you have staff that can be a headache just getting them to turn up on top of all the other problems you can have with staff. When you do take time off for a holiday or a break as long as you take a quick holiday maybe nobody will miss you but if you take extended time off your business will suffer.

If you work in an office on top of playing office politics if you want to take time off you may have to swop day shifts or week shifts with a colleague. And often with these jobs work never stops, you either have to take work home with you or if you are self employed customers are still ringing you at all hours and there's usually tons of paperwork to do. And often when you are not working you are still thinking about work and are never truly free from it.

You don't have any of these problems being a black cab driver there is no other job so flexible, London is open 24/7 so you can work around anything and make your own shifts up, if you are a morning person but don't like to work weekends no problem, if you hate mornings and prefer to work afternoons, evenings or nights no problem, if you prefer to mix it all up with any combination of hours there is no problem and if you take long periods of time off there are another 20,000 plus cabbies covering your shift so business doesn't suffer while you are not there and you can pick up where and whenever you like. The second you decide to go home you can immediately go home and once you are home your work has truly finished until you decide to go out again.

You can work as little or as long as you like. If you are a grafter you can work around the clock on the other hand if you are retired or semi retired it is an ideal job to work part time to top up your pension. The more you put in the more you get out.

There is no discrimination on the Knowledge; if you go to a Knowledge school you will find every nationality under the sun of both men and women. If you are a young mother and live in London you can work around the kids. Although traditionally a working class job there are no barriers to entry so there are black cabbies of all races, genders and class.

Another advantage of doing the Knowledge is as well as a test of topographical knowledge the Knowledge is also a test of character. It will be the hardest test most people will face in their lifetime with the exception of one or two courses you can do in the armed forces. So if you do make it through to the other side your character will have been fully tested going through all of the emotions and highs and lows of laughter, sadness, frustration, disappointment, elation etc.etc. In short you will come out the other side a better person. So what's stopping everybody from taking advantage of this prestige job? There is only one thing standing in your way; The Knowledge

There are black cab drivers from all walks of life, the job suits ex police, armed forces, firemen etc. because they have already had their character tested and usually have the discipline and determination to see it through, we also have ex professional footballers, boxers and all sorts of sports people but as I say the Knowledge is open to anybody and everybody that has the grit and determination to get through it. So if you are considering doing the Knowledge read this book crack on and get it started.

I have learnt that with all life skills that take years to accomplish like the Knowledge, foreign languages, martial arts etc that the most important thing about learning is attitude. You need to be positive and up for it as the saying goes "Whether you believe you can or whether you believe you can't you are right!"

Anything that takes a few years to learn many fall at the very first hurdle by making excuses not to do it saying it takes too long and not even starting. To overcome this I tell myself whether I do it or not the time is going to pass anyway with or without me, so if I decide not to do it the five years or whatever it is will pass anyway and then I will look back at the end of the five years and say to myself if I had started when I said I was going to start I would have reached my goal now! Some would be black cab drivers have learnt this lesson by starting the Knowledge with a friend. After a short time they give up and then a few years later they see their friend on Badge day just about to pick up a shiny new cab and start a new career. They could have had the same if only they had not given up. So take action and start your journey now if you haven't already done so.

On the Knowledge everybody's journey is different and personal to them due to age, where you live, your circumstances etc, so you should never compare yourself to others, your journey is unique and personal to you, however if you are finding the going tough but don't want to give up don't look at the best cabbies look at the worst ones, there is a very tiny minority of slobs that let the trade down, you know the ones I mean, dirty cabs and they look like they have been living in them, look at them and say to yourself if they can do it I can definitely do it, I absolutely refuse to accept they are better than me!

How to read this book

This book is aimed at a fairly wide audience, people who simply want to know what the Knowledge is and what it's all about, people thinking or contemplating about doing the Knowledge, Knowledge students of all levels, black cab drivers, anybody that is curious about what it was like to serve in the British army during the 1970's/80's before the world went crazy with political correctness, veterans that have served during this time and want to take a trip down memory lane, so the book is not necessarily designed to be read from cover to cover. For example if you are a cab driver or Knowledge student you will already be painfully aware of what the Knowledge is so you won't need to read the chapter explaining what the knowledge is or conversely if you have no idea what the Knowledge is and are just reading out of curiosity you may want to skip Knowledge chat about maps and places you've never heard of that maybe very boring unless you are a Knowledge student, in other words feel free to dip in and out wherever you like.

Chapter One

What is The Knowledge?

The black taxi trade can trace its roots back to Oliver Cromwell when he first licensed hackney carriages. Then moving forward to 1851 there was a world fair in Hyde Park they called The Great Exhibition. People came from all over the world. The exhibition was a great success apart from the cab drivers. The foreign guests were appalled at the cabbies complete lack of Knowledge and not having a clue where they were going. The story goes that Prince Albert was furious and said something along the lines of "we were proper mugged off by cabbies not knowing where they were going, this will NEVER happen in London again!!!" Not long after this the Knowledge was born. A test was made to test all cabbies by the police. As the test evolved it grew into the Knowledge that we know today. I always find it fascinating that when you watch a Jack the Ripper film and you see him in the film escape in a horse drawn cab into the foggy London night that cabbie taking Jack the Ripper will have done the Knowledge!

When you first register for the Knowledge you are invited to go to the Carriage Office for a meeting known as "The Talk". At the talk you are in a room with a small group of other students being told by a Knowledge examiner what to expect from the Knowledge and what is expected of you. I am told that back in the day they gave the talk in groups of ten and the examiner would say, "One of you will die, one of you will get divorced and between one and three of you will pass and the rest of you will fail, welcome to the Knowledge". I am told the prediction was pretty accurate. A friend of mine told me one of the students in his group on the talk got crushed by a lorry while he was out on his scooter.

Incidentally there is a saying in the cab trade that you cannot fail the Knowledge you can only give up. This is totally true the high percentage that "fail" do not fail at all they simply stop doing the Knowledge but if you keep going you will pass eventually. There are many people that have done the Knowledge that have a degree in fact some even have two degrees and they all say without exception that doing the Knowledge is harder than doing their degree(s), unlike a normal degree, on the Knowledge there is no end sight and you can also be put back as well as go forwards just like the classic game "Snakes and Ladders" but don't let any of this put you off the main quality you need is determination and the mindset not to give up. Remember you cannot fail only give up and if you don't give up you will get there it's as simple as that.

After the talk follows between a year and two years of self study. You are given a book called the "Blue Book". The blue book consists of lists of routes known as runs in Knowledge speak. There are 320 runs of which you are required to learn forwards and backwards and know them by heart. At the beginning and end of each run you are required to study a quarter of a mile radius. In these radii you must study every junction and make notes of road restrictions. Also you need to learn every building and point of interest known as points. Points are listed but not restricted as follows: Police stations, fire stations ambulance stations, schools, churches and places of worship, library's, pubs, bars, night clubs, hotels, train stations, bus stations, shops, department stores, embassies, town halls, civic halls, livery halls, any bloody halls, cinemas, museums, tourist attractions, leisure centres, theatres, hospitals, colleges, universities, criminal courts, cafes, restaurants, fast food outlets, ice cream parlours, prisons, art galleries, casinos, banks, gyms, hostels, markets, post offices, youth clubs and even the stage doors of theatres!

One examiner used to joke "If it's got a door on it I'll ask it!" but he forgot to say "If it hasn't got a door on it I'll ask it as well!" because you are also supposed to know but not restricted to the following: outdoor arenas, football stadiums, statues, graveyards, parks, outdoor events etc. In short anywhere where somebody will jump in the taxi and ask to go to. You are also supposed to pick up points along the runs as well although you don't need to do this because after you have done all 320 runs the quarter mile radii cover the whole of London like a giant jigsaw puzzle what's more they are not edge to edge they overlap so the points within them will cover all along the runs anyway. Also for this reason you only need to pick up just eight points in each radii for a few reasons. Firstly you can do too much in a study session, it's quality over quantity, the man who has done one run well backwards and forwards and has taken in everything he has seen and learnt is better than the man who has done ten runs but he can't "see" them properly and can't remember the points and has to do it all again because he has done too much in one study session. Secondly in a busy radius for example Australia House although eight points may not seem enough because there are obviously more than eight points within the radius when the radii overlap in this case with Aldwych, Surrey Street etc. the points multiply by eight with every radius so now we have twenty four points around Australia House with just the other two radii I have mentioned. With just eight points at the beginning and end of each run gives you a total of 320x 16= 5,120 points. Let me tell you that is an excellent start for the next stage and will stand you in very good stead for appearances and beyond, you will have a real solid foundation.

The next stage is called The Map Test. The map test is there to make sure you have studied your blue book and quarter mile radii properly and are ready for appearances and aren't going to waste the examiners and your time by not being ready. The map test is also there so they have something to put you back to if you fail your 56 day appearances and get "red lined" (Red lined will be explained further into the book).

Before you do the map test you are invited by the Carriage Office to do a voluntary mock map test. On the voluntary map test the scores are not recorded in fact you take your exam paper with you after you have finished the mock test and the Carriage Office doesn't even see it. The idea is to give you a feel for the real map test and for you to see your own progress at this early stage. Although no scores are recorded or kept your attendance is recorded. There's a clue there. From the moment you are registered on the Knowledge they are building and keeping a file on you. If I were head examiner I would make sure all the examiners knew on a candidates first appearance who was keen and taking things seriously by attending the voluntary map test and who couldn't be bothered to turn up for the voluntary map test when invited. I have seen students on Knowledge forums just before the map test panicking and asking everybody what to expect. If they had bothered to go to the voluntary map test they would know. I can tell you the voluntary map test is exactly the same as the real map test, albeit different points and runs of course.

The map test is the easiest test you will do on the knowledge and the only test where you will be holding a pen, it's just a multi choice tick box test that you will find really easy if you did your blue book runs and quarter miles properly. The questions are a few runs that have a run that has an illegal turn and another that is obviously wide and one that is correct; you just mark the one that is correct. It then goes onto points. It gives a point and then gives you multi choice addresses; obviously you mark the box that has the correct address. The pass mark is 60%. You get the result through the post and/or email in a few days time along with the date of your first appearance if you pass. If you fail you have to take it again. Remember you might fail the map test or individual appearances but you can't fail the Knowledge you can only give up. Doing my blue book properly with eight points on each radius I found the map test very easy and scored 90%. Appearances weren't to prove so easy for me.

Completing your blue books is a lot of work and an achievement in itself but they say the Knowledge doesn't really start until you are on appearances. Appearances are one to one examinations with a Knowledge of London examiner.

There are three stages of appearances 56's, 28's, and 21's so called because you appear every 56 days and then when you are good enough you get your drop (see Knowledge speak at the back of the book) and move up to the next stage and then you appear every 28 days and so on until you go all the way through 21's and finally get that hand shake and your req and have finished the knowledge of London. At this stage you have passed but it's not quite over yet, you now have to go away and study the suburb runs for your final exam. The suburb runs are the main arteries in and out of the outskirts of London and cover all the terminals of Heathrow airport. The final examination is one last appearance tested on the suburbs this appearance is slightly less formal and should be an easy appearance if you have done the work. The examiners still want to see that you have done the work and people do fail it and have to take it again so just make sure like everything on the Knowledge that you do it properly. After the suburbs there is an advanced driving test called "The Drive" and then after passing that you are a fully qualified London cab driver and you go to the Carriage Office for a badge presentation where you collect your badge and new licence (known as your bill) and then candidates usually go straight from the badge presentation to their chosen taxi garage to pick up a cab and then they are ready to start work. You are now known as a butter boy (a new fresh driver) and it is customary to give away your first fare free. After my Badge day on the Friday I went on my first shift early evening on the following day. I turned on my light on Borough High Street travelling northbound. My first fare was a group of German tourists that hailed me on King William Street and wanted to go to Sloane Square. A nice run to get me started, we were chatting on the journey and it turned out one of the passengers home town in Germany was where I was stationed for a couple of years in the army, it's a small world. When we got to Sloane Square they wanted to pay me with a good tip on top, I had quite a job persuading them that I didn't want paying but they eventually agreed when I told them I'm very superstitious and believed I would have bad luck for the rest of my new career if I accepted payment so they eventually went on their way wishing me the best of luck. As they left a lady got in immediately going to Cumberland Street nearby in Pimlico (There was nobody on the Sloane Square rank so it was OK to take her). The night continued one in and one out, a great start to my new career.

When Cabbies go out for the first time after badge day some are a bit nervous or apprehensive about putting their light on for the very first time but you quickly go from that to wanting to beat yourself up because you have forgot to put your light on! and have been driving around busy areas wondering why nobody wants to hail you!

Chapter Two

Sat Nav Versus The Knowledge

When you start the Knowledge you will quickly regret telling people that you are on the Knowledge because although they know it takes years to finish every time they see you they will still say " are you still on the Knowledge?" this can be very annoying especially after you have just had a bad appearance.

Another annoying thing is people will forever be saying, "what about sat nav?" (What about it?) or "Do people still need to do the Knowledge now they have sat nav?"

Just in case you are a reader outside of the trade I will explain. Sat nav like all computers is only as good as the information or data that is put into it.

Firstly if sat nav was as good as the Knowledge we wouldn't be studying for years doing the Knowledge we would just buy a sat nav and save ourselves years of hard study. Sat nav is actually trying to be like us and not the other way around, some apps have followed black cabbies routes and have put them into their own data.

Consider this, imagine somebody has come to London who has never been to London ever before. Now you are going to race that person to your house and all he has to rely on is sat nav and a postcode. Who do you think is going to win that race?

You will win it every time because not only do you know exactly where you are going you will change the route to suit the traffic and time of day (or night), you will also be driving more confidently and safely. In fact many media people have tested black cabs against sat nav many times over the years and sat nav has always come a very sorry second.

As black cab drivers we also have many places we can drive that ordinary traffic cannot for example bus lanes, Oxford Street, banned turns etc and there are even streets we know about that are not even on any map and a sat nav will not know any of this. Sometimes when I am driving a nice tight Knowledge route across Soho the customer in the back with their sat nav on is surprised I'm not going the same way as the sat nav and I have to explain that the sat nav doesn't know we are a London black taxi and is doing it's best to keep us off of Oxford Street thereby taking us all around the houses on an unnecessarily long route!

Sat nav is generally rubbish in central London due to road closures that can literally change by the hour. The sat nav can't calculate very recent road closures quick enough but with the Knowledge we can work around it no problem at all. Quite often we get mini cab drivers coming towards us the wrong way down a one way street because the sat nav has told them to. Some of these drivers even know they are going the wrong way but they don't know where to go so instead

they have to knowingly go the wrong way or otherwise go in completely the wrong direction. So sat nav can be very dangerous in London. It may be OK as a one off for an amateur to take a mate somewhere but if you use an app based mini cab they are supposed to be professional drivers.

Many points we get asked to go to have no signage and the customer wants to be dropped off right outside the door for example there are hundreds of private members clubs in London with no signs, we learn where all the doors are. Sat nav might get you to a theatre eventually but it won't know where the stage door is, we learn where the stage doors are to every theatre, sat nav cannot tell you any of this.

On the Knowledge after you have finished your blue books you start point to point. Point to point is calculating any two points across London using the shortest possible route. You spend years doing this all through the appearance stages. As a complete beginner on point to point sometimes with a hard route you think to yourself "I know I'll "cheat" and see what the sat nav says" after seeing an outrageously bad route you quickly learn to forget about sat nav and are reminded why you are studying the Knowledge.

Having said all of that sat nav does have its place as a cab driver. On my finals the examiner said to me sat nav on it's own is OK (sometimes), the Knowledge on it's own is very good but if you put the two together you have a killer combination. When I am driving my cab I have the A-Z app running most of the time, I'm not following it on the contrary I have the tracker on so it's following me! I have it on because it's useful when you are in a residential area and all the roads look the same especially at night in the dark, for example the Haringey Ladder you can see when your exact turning is coming up.

When somebody asks for a new restaurant or something and we have to Google it, it's not the same for a London black cab diver googling as it is anybody else Googling it because a normal member of the public Google's it and they still have to find it but when we Google something we only need to see one inch of the map and we know exactly where it is and we can see in our mind the quickest route to it from wherever we are and we are off!

Chapter Three

Getting Started

The first thing you will need is a mode of transport to do your runs, go pointing and then when you are on appearances go back and look at points and junctions that are not clear to you.

Without doubt the best form of transport for this is a scooter with a clipboard on the front to clip your maps to. The advantages of a scooter are that they are very cheap to run on fuel, insurance etc and there is no congestion charge. Another advantage is you can get everywhere filtering congested traffic and also U turn in the road really easy. You also have unrestricted vision with a scooter with no roof or panels to get in the way when you are looking at buildings and high places. The main disadvantage of a scooter is the cold in winter. A good investment is heated grips.

Today most people choose a Smart car over a scooter because the main advantages are you can stay toast warm in a car and you are also much safer from traffic accidents, pot holes and crime. However if you are going to choose a car make sure it is congestion charge free and if possible it has a panoramic roof so you can see more.

If you choose a scooter a Honda is the scooter of choice, you will be doing a phenomenal amount of miles and a Honda will keep going forever, reliability is everything on the Knowledge.

I live in Kent and am forty two miles from Leicester Square. I did all of my Knowledge on a scooter until I got to 21's then I switched to a big four wheeled drive car because I knew I was finishing and would be driving a cab soon so I wanted to get a feel for driving the streets in the closest thing I could get to a cab.

I was lucky to be able to study the Knowledge full time I was also lucky to have a full bike licence so I could ride my scooter on the M25. I say lucky to have a full bike licence because it was virtually given to me in February 1981 when I was in the army. The troop sergeant said to me, "Cabman! How many wheels has a motorcycle got! ?"

Me "errrm…. Two Sergeant (?)"

Troop Sergeant "You seem to know a lot about motorcycles Cabman, here's your licence."

Of course I am exaggerating a little but not much. The army bike test in 1981 consisted of a week's course. Day one was riding around a few cones on camp and then riding at walking pace in a straight line next to the walking corporal instructor we then did a hill start on a slight incline on camp and then the next few days were riding around camp and the surrounding area and test day on the Friday. The test consisted of riding up the dual carriageway just up the road from camp with the corporal instructor until we got into the local town centre, we then just had to ride around the block until we met the testing Sergeant on the street corner of the block who then put his hand in the air that was a signal to do an emergency stop, he then asked us a few road signs from the highway code book he was holding and then informed us that we had passed and were now full bike licence holders.

After this day in February 1981 I never ever rode a bike again until I started the Knowledge in June 2014.

Riding up the M25 most days from Kent I wore out two brand new bikes although it has to be said I didn't take my own advice and buy a Honda otherwise I probably would have only needed one. When buying a scooter for the Knowledge you also have to take into consideration how often it needs servicing. There was no Honda dealer near where I live in Kent hence me choosing something a bit more inferior. Whatever scooter I chose was always going to need regular servicing thrashing it up the M25 so I needed a local garage that could keep me on the road.

When I started The Knowledge in 2014 there were knowledge students on bikes everywhere. Virtually every point you visited there was already a Knowledge student there or one would arrive as you were pulling away. Then after about a year I noticed less and less as time went on. I noticed the roads were getting a lot more potholes so it was getting more dangerous especially when it got dark in the winter. I did my bike work all through the winters using my army mentality of not making any allowances for the weather. Whenever I was riding up the motorway in the freezing winter I would think to myself that if I were back in the army, instead of having a bike I would just have a pair of black leather boots and instead of having a clearly marked A-Z I would have an old ordnance survey map and a compass to navigate from and finally if I were back in the army and somebody said to me go out on your bike for the day it wouldn't matter how cold it was I would be thinking to myself What's the catch? Because it would be like somebody sending you on a skiving holiday. These thoughts kept me going.

However I did change my thinking eventually after going out one day on a run to Muswell Hill. Muswell Hill is the furthest run from my house. It was torrential rain before I left and the forecast was it was going to continue to at least the next day. I put on my waterproofs over my armoured bike suit and off I went. As soon as I got to the motorway despite my waterproofs it was as if somebody had thrown me in a lake but I kept going all the way to Muswell Hill regardless. On my way up I was thinking of a Knowledge student that had put on the forum asking where were the best places to pullover for a brew and a warm up and for me it was a sip of cold water on the hard shoulder of the motorway. I did all of my work in Muswell Hill but I couldn't see everything clearly and all of my notes were soaked so I had to do the work again at a later date. I decided that I wasn't in the army anymore and could be a bit more sensible with my seven P's. The seven P's are army slang and they mean "Perfect planning and preparation prevents piss poor performance"

I still think riding a scooter is the best way to do the Knowledge so if you are going to do the Knowledge on a scooter I will offer some safety advice. This is not aimed at seasoned bikers but more at very young inexperienced riders or maybe office workers or people that have never ridden a bike before. I don't want to tell your grandmother how to suck eggs so if you are an experienced rider you may want to skip this and move onto the next chapter. I make no apologies for including it because if it makes just one person think and saves a life or prevents somebody from getting hurt it would have made writing the whole book worth it, so here goes.....

As I say I do hold a full bike licence but considering I hadn't even sat on a bike for over thirty years between passing my test and doing the

Knowledge to say I was rusty would be the understatement of the year. So if you have never ridden a bike before I respectfully suggest you do what I did and go out at four a.m and have a good ride around the streets with no traffic around until you get used to it. When there were loads of Knowledge students on bikes I never saw one that wasn't wearing high viz so it's hardly worth mentioning here however I did notice a lot of courier riders and some Knowledge students wearing "high viz" that was so dirty that they "weren't" wearing high viz. The congestion on the roads is so bad that it can turn high viz to black in a very short period of time. When I went to replace my high viz I was surprised how cheap it is, you can find it on e bay for the price of a cup of coffee so my tip is to replace it every week it really could save your life. The biggest danger to me on my bike before Uber came along was other bikers. When on your bike please look over your shoulder before making any manoeuvre, I was shocked at the amount of bikers that just use their mirrors and don't bother to look over their shoulder when moving out of filtered traffic. When filtering stationery congested traffic bikes in front of me would pull out in front of me nearly colliding with me so I had a rule of not passing other bikers in congested traffic. And I know for a fact Knowledge students have been crushed filtering on the inside of lorries so it's always worth a reminder even if it is common sense. I had a good friend of mine get knocked off his bike by a van and went sliding across the road on his chin luckily he was wearing a full face crash helmet with the visor down so his chin was saved but if he had been wearing an open face helmet he wouldn't have a chin today. I would always bear this in mind when I pulled up to a point and lifted my visor, I would always make sure I lowered it again before pulling away. As I spent a lot of time on the road including the motorway I would always wear bike armour, gloves and motorcycle boots, in the summer it is extremely tempting not to bother but if you are like me and have seen the damage that's done to your body and your life if you come off with no protection it's handy to know you can get light weight versions of the protective armour especially for the summer months. Another big danger on London roads are drivers that don't hold a UK driving licence. When you are at a roundabout and they have stopped but it is THEIR

23

right of way and they are sitting there not knowing who's right of way it is and they are waving for you to go when it is their right of way you know for sure they didn't get their driving licence in the UK. When riding a bike you should always assume you are invisible in other words that other traffic hasn't seen you. When passing side streets even though it was my right of way I would always slow down and assume the vehicle pulling out hadn't seen me I would only proceed when I was sure they had seen me. Some of the Uber drivers are without doubt some of the most dangerous drivers on the road they were so bad that along with the extra potholes appearing everywhere influenced my decision to eventually switch to a car when I was on 21's. Hopefully by the time you are reading this things will have improved.

Chapter Four

The Games Dead

Soon after you start doing your runs it won't be long before an ageing cabbie comes along side you and says something along the lines of "Give up son you're wasting your time, this games had it, the games dead!"

It goes without saying you should ignore these negative people however you may wonder to yourself why they say it.

There are actually many reasons. The first one is it's traditional. Ever since the trade started cabbies have been saying it to Knowledge students. All of the old timers will tell you that they heard it when they were doing the Knowledge and you can hear it in the excellent 1979 film "The Knowledge" written by Jack Rosenthal. Incidentally you can get the film on Amazon or you can watch it for free on You Tube. I believe Oliver Cromwell probably said it when he gave out the first Hackney Carriage licence!

So some of the cabbies that say it to you are only saying it because it was said to them.

The second reason is, way back in the day many cabbies had done military service and anyone that's served will tell you that when you are in basic training and at your lowest, soaking wet through, having not eaten or slept a member of the training staff will approach you and whisper in your ear, "you don't have to do this son, give up now, go and get yourself a nice brew and you can be on the next train home". It's all part of the training and they only want people to get through that can handle it and who deserve it, it's a way of sorting out the wheat from the chaff, the men from the boys and getting rid of the weak. Some old cabbies will see themselves as helping the examiners with their character testing.

A third reason is there are not many jobs where council estate working class people can do a rewarding job and in the golden years of the cab trade the financial rewards were considered reasonably good for the working class. Old cabbies being well aware of this wanted to "protect" the trade, they didn't want it to become like mini cabs where it was saturated so much it would become hard to make it worthwhile let alone get a living so they saw themselves as the gatekeepers and tried to put off as many people as possible. What they didn't seem to realise is that black cab numbers are capped and controlled anyway unlike mini cabs where literally anybody can be one that hands over money. What's more the trade already has its gatekeepers they are called Knowledge of London examiners. Ironically there's only one thing that will make the game dead and that is no Knowledge students coming through.

The fourth reason they say it is because they are telling the truth but they are telling you THEIR truth not YOUR truth. I'll explain; when you finish the Knowledge and finally get in a cab you are out all of the time, working long hours and of course being paid accordingly. After a while you say to yourself I don't need to work all of these hours I can afford to have a day or two off. Then when you are out working you say to yourself I don't need to be rushing around all the time while I am working I'll go in the café and have a break and then over a long period of time the working hours are getting shorter and the breaks are getting longer until one day you are sitting in a cabbie café with your mates saying I don't earn the money I used to and then your mate will say it's funny you should say that because neither do I and then you will both conclude the games dead. So be aware and don't become one of these lazy negative cabbies.

As I have already said you should ignore these cabbies really but I always used to have some stock answers ready to fire back at these negative cabbies. In truth I never needed them maybe it's because I'm a bit older and they preferred to pick on younger students or maybe they could sense that I had some answers ready for them. Not to waste them I told the younger students what to say. The obvious one to say is "My dad/brother is a cabbie" or alternatively for emphasis you could say "I come from a cabbie family, my dad, brothers and uncles are all cabbies". Or if you really want to wind them up you could say, "I've just sold my internet company and don't need to work I'm just doing this to keep myself occupied and then when I have finished I will just nip out weekends and nick a bit of your work". They love that one ha ha.

Seriously as a cabbie to protect the trade you should do the exact opposite of what the doom and gloomers do, you should go out of your way to actively encourage Knowledge students because they are the life and blood of the trade. Without Knowledge students coming through the trade will die. Like anything elite the Knowledge is never safe from the Marxist left, they absolutely despise anything that has high standards and is elite and will always try to ban it or at least sabotage it, if they can't ban it they will try to dumb it down. Political correctness is also the enemy of high standards. So whenever I see a Knowledge student out on their bike working hard I always pull up alongside them wind my window down and say something along the lines of "Keep going, don't give up!" and then if they want a chat I try to give them all the advice and encouragement I can.

Chapter Five

The Blue Book

When I was thinking for a title for this book I was going to call it "The Knowledge Bible". Anybody that's done the Knowledge will know that that would have been a diabolical liberty because there is only one bible on the Knowledge and it's called "The Blue Book"

Nobody seems to know why it's called the blue book because it was actually pink for a few years. My personal belief taking an educated guess is on account of the Metropolitan Police running the Knowledge for so many years is that it was probably blue at one stage during the knowledge's long history but that is unconfirmed it's just my guess and probably wrong.

The blue book consists of 320 runs that consist of a start point and an end point and you are to work out the quickest route between the two points of each run. Like all runs on the Knowledge you do this by marking both points start and finish on a large wall map, you then join the two points with a straight line as the crow flies either by using a ruler and a dry marker pen or more traditionally a piece of string or cotton with a lump of blu tack at each end so the string can be pulled tight and secured and then moved around the map with ease. You then mark the route with a dry wipe pen using roads that keep as close to the string as possible without any illegal moves like banned turns or going up a no entry for example.

You will be pleased to know that the Knowledge schools have already done this work for you so you can buy your blue books from a Knowledge school with the best routes already worked out for you with no illegal's. You will notice that I said blue book in the plural this is because the schools have split the blue book into four with eighty runs in each book.

The first blue book run is Manor House Station to Gibson Square. This run has almost iconic status because on account of it being the very first run everybody knows it including the tens of thousands of people that have started the Knowledge and never finished it and those of us that have finished that's the run we have called the most on account of it being the first run.

You are also asked to learn the runs backwards but as a beginner I would just concentrate on learning them forwards at first and then worry about learning them backwards when you have finished your blue books because by then it will be more of a case of tweaking them rather than learning them.

After you have completed a run you have to call it out loud road by road. When you call the run you don't just learn it parrot fashion you have to "see" the roads in your mind so every time you call the run it is the next best thing to driving it that's why it's so important to actually go there and drive the route taking your time and taking everything in so that you will be able to see the roads when you call them.

Everybody that starts the Knowledge says to themselves, "Right! I'm going to smash this thing out in the fastest possible time" If you want to make God laugh tell him your plans come into mind! It is natural and typical human nature to want to find a "fast way" cut corners or find a shortcut. I did find one shortcut on the Knowledge and it is this: Do it properly the first time and you will not have to do it again. Doing it once is a short cut doing it twice being sent back to map test etc is not. Another well worn saying on the Knowledge is; "It's a marathon not a sprint"

In other words pace yourself accordingly. On a marathon you wouldn't start by running as fast as you possibly can because you would be so out of breath you wouldn't be able to carry on let alone finish, the Knowledge is no different so take your time and remember quality over quantity at all times.

Here's another good piece of advice I wish somebody had told me when I started: Don't apply to register for the Knowledge until you have done at least one blue book. The reason being once you have been accepted on the Knowledge you have exactly two years to put in for your map test, if the time expires and you have not put in for your map test you are off the Knowledge. Two years may sound like a long time but it soon goes and if anything unfortunate comes up in your life two years is not enough it's better to give yourself a generous buffer because you can always put in for your map test early if you are ready but if you are not ready you will have to put in for an extension of time to finish your blue books. In my case I didn't register for the Knowledge until after I had completed thirty runs with hindsight I would have given myself more time by registering on the Knowledge later. On the early days of my runs somehow somewhere I picked up a DVT (blood clot) in my right leg. My right leg swelled up like a balloon and delayed me for a good few weeks, luckily I had done those thirty runs beforehand but it would have been more comfortable time wise if I had done more than thirty runs before registering for the Knowledge. I wouldn't have let a minor detail like losing a leg allow me to give up the Knowledge and I was already thinking how I could adapt a Smart car and later a cab to drive with one leg. Luckily I made a full recovery and none of that was needed but it does illustrate the mindset you need to complete the Knowledge.

You have to call your blue book runs everyday seeing the routes and roads as you call them. Another good idea is to pen the runs up on the map with a dry marker because ultimately you are trying to get the A-Z map burnt into your memory. Every London cabbie can see the A-Z in detail in their mind and that only comes with years looking at the map and penning up runs. As a beginner you need to call every run you have done up to eighty runs every day and then when you have done over eighty runs continue calling eighty a day. Some people stop calling their blue book when they get onto 21's and some even stop calling it on 28's but I believe this is a big mistake you should never stop! I called my blue book up to suburbs and then stopped calling it as a cab driver but I still brush over ten runs a day with points if I am off work for any length of time. When you are an intermediate student when you close your eyes you will begin to see parts of the A-Z map in your mind and when you are an advanced student as you are calling your runs you will see a mixture of the actual real life roads and a mixture of the A-Z map.

As the Knowledge takes a few years to complete it stands to reason you will have bad luck as well as good luck in your day to day life. In other words you will be very lucky to get through it without having a personal set back somewhere along the way. Many students on the Knowledge have got a "Hard luck" story. Some have been laid up in hospital after coming off of their scooter. Some have had to go through a divorce and a fair few have had to fight terminal illness and countless students have lost close family members. All of this adds to the pressure and makes the tough Knowledge journey even tougher.

My own personal "hard luck" story besides getting a DVT (Deep Vein Thrombosis) was that my dear old mum was diagnosed with lung cancer and given six months to live not long after I had started the Knowledge. My mum was of strong character and was just as determined to see me get my badge as I was. It took me over four years to pass the Knowledge and my mum managed to hang on until I got my Req. Getting towards the end my wife could see the end was coming better than I could as I was focusing on the Knowledge and I also thought my mum would go on forever. So my wife encouraged me to go around and visit her every Saturday. Every time I passed an appearance I would text my mum on the train home and she later told me it gave her a real boost and helped her to hang on. She loved the Saturday visits and would test me on the suburb runs. I don't recommend current students be tested on their runs by somebody who is not on the Knowledge as they won't be able to see or correct your mistakes but in this case it was a special case as it made my mum feel like she was helping me and we were getting the last precious moments together also the suburb runs are set in stone so it's easier for a layman to test you.

I never mentioned my mum to anybody at the Carriage Office ever. The examiners have got a job to do and I don't think it's fair on them to burden them with our own personal problems, also I didn't want them to think I was looking for some kind of sympathy or making excuses for a bad appearance.

My mum passed away four days before my final exam. I was grateful that she managed to hang on and see me get my Req but the timing wasn't ideal. I was devastated and had to do my final exam in four days time. We are a close family and the family all agreed that my mum would have wanted me to stay focused and pass the final exam so that's exactly what I did. I managed to hide what I had been through from the examiner entirely. I will always be grateful to my wife for encouraging me to visit my mum regularly towards the end of my Knowledge journey and towards the end of my mum's life.

Chapter Six

Pointing

When you do your quarter mile radii you will need to know how to point properly. When you arrive at a new point the first thing to note is where the door of the point is. You will then need to know how to set down the point (arrive and park up for the customer to get out) and how to leave the point, what's more you will need to know how to do this from all directions.

Where possible you always set down on the left (SDOL) this is because the wheelchair ramp is on the left hand side of the vehicle.

Let's start with an easy point The Imperial War Museum on Lambeth Road. You can certainly SDOL and there's nothing stopping you from travelling up Lambeth Road eastbound and pulling over to the right hand side of the road and setting down on the right (SDOR). Whenever you SDOR if there's a small traffic island in the middle of the road under

Knowledge rules this can be ignored but if there was a central reservation or some other obstruction it would be impossible to SDOR. With this point it's equally easy to leave on the left (LOL) or again you could leave it from the right hand side of the road facing east (LOR). Sometimes you will need to explain to an examiner or a call over partner which side of the road a point is on so you should immediately get out of the habit of saying it's on the left hand side or it's on the right hand side because if a point is on your left hand side when you turn around it is now on your right hand side and vice versa so to avoid confusion use something that never changes instead, what never change are compass points. The Imperial War Museum is on the South side of Lambeth Road this never changes it doesn't matter if it's on your left hand side or your right hand side it is and is always south.

So your notes for The Imperial War museum would look something like this:

Imperial War Museum NRS (No Restrictions)

Lambeth Road (S)

LOL LOR

SDOL SDOR

The Imperial War Museum is classed as an easy point because it is NRS. Now let's try a slightly trickier point. The Adelphi Theatre on Strand. Now because of the central reservation going all the way up the strand this point is LOL SDOL only. For leaving if you are going east there is no problem but if you need to go west you will need a turn around (T/A) or in Knowledge slang a spin. In real life you would simply do a U turn and on the Strand there is a small gap in the central reservation just east of the Adelphi Theatre so you can do just that however on the Knowledge U turns are prohibited. The reason U turns are prohibited is that you need to learn all roads on the Knowledge so each T/A usually needs on average three roads to turn around so that's three roads you have learnt and memorised instead of doing a U turn. Even if there are no points on the T/A people probably live there and may simply ask the street to go home and you wouldn't know it if you hadn't learnt the T/A. For this point you have the same problem for setting, again it's fine if you are coming from the west but if you are coming from the east you will need to learn a T/A

So your notes for the Adelphi Theatre will look like this:

Adelphi Theatre

Strand (N)

LOL SDOL Only

T/A LOL Strand L Burleigh St L &L Exeter St R Strand

To set from East F Strand comply King Charles Island Lby (Leave by) Trafalger Square eastside R Duncannon St L Strand SDOL   Note: you can T/A in Charing Cross Station Forecourt ask examiner permission to do so.

Now you know how to point properly you will need to collect as many points as is humanly possible, you can never have too many points on the Knowledge and you will not stop collecting them until the very end. Once you have collected a point you will need to catalogue it along with your notes of how to set and leave from all directions and any restrictions. How you catalogue it is entirely up to the individual many youngsters these days use apps and some people put them on cards and then store the cards in boxes. Once you have found a way to catalogue them that suits you, you will then need to find a way of revising them. I used to revise my points alongside calling my blue book. I used to take a photograph of every point I collected, as I am a visual thinker it helped me to memorize my points. While I was out pointing and photographing a building or the restrictions on a junction I was always surprised by paranoid security guards that would come out and try and tell me I was doing something wrong while I was going about my normal legal business. If you like to take photos while you are out pointing it helps to know where you stand legally because I found out from experience most "security" guards didn't have the first clue of the laws on street photography and would wrongly assume it was illegal to photograph where they worked, so here goes: If you are on public land and not causing an obstruction you may photograph any public or private building, person (including the police) or animal, basically if you can see it you can shoot it. If you step onto private land the landowner can ask you not to take photographs for example some cinemas, theatres and shopping malls ask you not to take photos on their private land. So if you are on the public street taking a photo of a pub for example nobody can stop you but the minute you go into the pubs private car park to take the same photo you may be asked to stop. Members of the public appearing in these photos is not illegal, but the law changes if you are going to sell them or publish them so it shouldn't interfere with your Knowledge work. Nobody has the power to delete your images without a court order. The police should never delete your images because if they were illegal they would want to keep them as evidence and if they are perfectly legal they have no right to delete them. Security guards have no legal right to interfere with your camera or delete images. As I say it's good to know where you stand with over the top busy bodies but if you use common sense you shouldn't have any problems, good luck and keep snapping those points!

On some very busy junctions and red routes sometimes I found it difficult to set down and take a photo so I invested in a waterproof camera and hung it from the loop on my wrist and then when I was stuck in traffic or waiting at a red light I could take a photo of a point at a seconds notice and then literally drop the camera as the lights went green.

No point on the Knowledge is a waste of time. Sometimes I found myself pointing some obscure bowls club in the back streets of a residential area and just as I was thinking to myself what a waste of time this is, who is going to ask to get a cab here? A black cab would arrive, pull up and a customer would get out right in front of me, so I was being proved wrong in real time. You might find on the Knowledge that a residential street just has one point on it, maybe a tennis club or a scout hut or something, as a working cabbie nobody may ever ask for these points but the rest of the buildings on the street are houses so somebody may definitely ask for one of those on their way home from work or a night out in town and the tennis club or scout hut will help you remember the name of the street. There is always a clever reason for everything on the Knowledge.

Chapter Seven

Runs and Points together or Separately?

There are two recognised ways of doing the Knowledge the first one as explained previously studying a quarter mile radius followed by the run and then studying the end point radius, this is known as the "dumbbell effect" because if you draw a circle on the map (quarter mile radius) and then a straight line (the run) to the next circle it will resemble a dumbbell.

The second method is to do all 320 runs first and then do all 640 quarter mile radii after you have completed all 320 runs. There are pros and cons with both methods but which one you choose is entirely up to the individual. Both methods work and both methods will get you your badge but it's more up to the quality of the student than the method of completing your blue books.

The two main long established Knowledge schools in London are Knowledge Point School and Wizann Knowledge School. Knowledge Point School teaches the dumbbell effect and Wizann teaches runs and points separately. Do not waste your time getting into the negative stupidity of arguing which method is best or which school is best you will need all of your time and energy to study the Knowledge. Both schools do a free beginners introductory talk so good advice is to go to both and see which school and method suits you best, everybody is different and has different life circumstances so what may suit one person may not work for another person and vice versa.

I do not claim to be a Knowledge expert but I will attempt to explain the pros and cons of each method.

Firstly the dumbbell effect. The pros are that while you are in the area anyway doing your run you may as well pick up a few points while you are there. An advantage of pointing from day one is that blue book runs crisscross each other so you are getting maximum revision every time you pass a point you have already pointed and at the end of completing your blue books you will have a minimum of 5,120 points. Doing a few points with each run makes it easy to revise your points while calling your blue book. In some of the later blue books some of the runs will almost repeat themselves so it might be tempting to cheat and not do them but the Knowledge is all about repetition and with this method it's impossible to cheat because after you have pointed the first radius of the run you can't point the second radius until you have completed the run! When I did my map test I got 90% because virtually all the points on the map test were in my Knowledge point school blue book. The main disadvantage of this method is that it does seem a very hard slog and slow going and some beginners find it hard taking in points as well as trying to memorize runs at this very early stage of the Knowledge.

Moving onto the second method. The main advantage of this method is doing the runs on their own you can do them relatively quickly and hitting the milestone of completing your runs so soon gives you the feeling you are making good progress and any positive encouragement on the Knowledge is always welcome. Another advantage is after completing 320 runs you will know your way around the whole of London so you won't be getting lost whilst out pointing. A potential disadvantage of doing too many runs too fast is that they all merge into one and if you're not careful you may have to go and do them again if you can't see the roads properly when calling. The downside to doing your runs so quickly is you now have the daunting task of doing 640 quarter mile radii. Many students under estimate how many points they need for each stage. Doing your quarter miles separately it is very tempting not to do them all. This method works if you do what's asked of you and you do it properly. If you choose this method make sure you have enough points 5000 is a good number to get you comfortably through the map test and even all the way through 56's. An advantage of doing your Quarter mile radii separately is that you do them by postcode and doing them by postcode gives you good postcode knowledge.

When I did the Knowledge being an old school type of guy I did the whole of the Knowledge without technology. I went out on my bike with the A-Z map and my runs and points clipped on my Knowledge board, I only used maps and pens the only "technology" I used was a biro instead of a pencil, a camera for taking photos of points and restrictions on junctions and a Dictaphone for taking down my notes if it was raining, I also used the Dictaphone for the later stage of point to point between call over partners.

Both Knowledge Schools now have their own apps so when choosing a school it might be an idea to look at both school apps to see which one suits you best.

You should attend Knowledge schools and call over clubs as much as you possibly can, time and money permitting. Schools and call over clubs give you the best chance of using varied call over partners which is a big advantage than calling over with just one person, the more call over partners the better.

Chapter Eight

Point to Point

Your blue book is your solid foundation. Although it's possible a passenger might jump in your cab and ask for a blue book run, the vast majority of routes asked although they may have a part of a blue book run in there somewhere will be something different so therefore to be a London black cab driver you will need to wean yourself off of the blue book but that's not to say you should neglect it far from it you should still be calling it everyday. The way you wean yourself off of the blue book runs is point to point.

The first thing you will need for point to point is a large wall map of the A-Z the bigger the better. The best pens to use are Nobo liquid ink dry markers and the best thing to clean the map with is magic sponge which you can buy in any supermarket but you can get them cheaper online or from the pound shop. You will also need a long piece of string with a lump of blu tack at each end.

For point to point a good call over partner (cop) is essential. You can do it without a call over partner but it's very hard going doing it without one. I found it better calling over with cops that went to a different Knowledge school than myself this was because the blue book runs differ slightly from school to school and you are able to show each other things that you may not have seen before. If you have just finished your blue books now would be an excellent time to learn them backwards as a good and useful way of easing into point to point. You will hear some students say that you don't need to learn them backwards but trust me it's an absolute game changer, it opens the map right up for you and there is at least one examiner that likes to ask blue book runs backwards. So with your back to the map call Gibson Square to Manor House Station. As you are calling your call over partner will be penning the run up on the map in real time as you are calling it. Before you started calling your call over partner (Cop) will have secured the string between the two points. If you do not have a cop call your run into a Dictaphone. After calling your run see how close your call was to the string, a wide call we call a banana because that's the shape it generally resembles on the map. If your call wasn't good pen up what it should have been and call it again, with your back to the map of course. When you have called a run you are happy with it's then your cop's turn to call and your turn to pen up. Penning up for your cop is just as valuable to you as calling over because you are seeing the map and ultimately you want to see the whole map in your mind without looking at it.

On a call over session it's traditional to call each other Sir and you will notice all the students in the Knowledge schools and call over clubs call each other and everybody Sir this is because in appearances you call the examiners Sir or if the examiner is female Maam and you want to make the call over sessions as near to an appearance as you can. On appearances the examiners like you to call them Sir not just out of respect but they want you to transfer this over to paying customers when you eventually get in your cab, likewise they like to see you very smart at appearances so although they know you are not going to wear a suit to work but if after finishing the Knowledge you dress 60% as smart as an appearance you will still be smart and presentable enough to drive a cab.

Usually you call four runs each that's because on every appearance the examiner asks you four runs. When the question is asked either by your cop or an examiner on an appearance think of your line first and then start calling steadily and confidently there are no extra points for calling too fast in fact there is at least one examiner that stops you and asks you to start again if you call too fast, remember the person penning or the examiner are trying to follow your line so if you call too fast it makes their job more difficult. When doing point to point if you are a similar level as your cop then calling four runs each is fine but if one of you is a beginner and taking too long thinking of your line and then taking ages to call it maybe getting mind blanks then a fairer system is to use a timer. An appearance is around fifteen to twenty minutes so give each other fifteen minutes each to call a maximum of four runs, if you don't get up to four change over anyway this system allows both students to get the maximum out of a call over session. To make call over as near to an appearance as possible it helps to have as many call over partners as possible two heads are better than one but eight heads are better than two! You can learn something from all cops even if they are at a lower level. Knowledge schools and call over clubs are invaluable for introducing you to new cops.

When you get onto appearances as soon as you leave the building after your appearance there will be people from the knowledge schools with clipboards waiting for you to go over to them and tell them what points and runs the examiner asked you on your appearance, these people are known as point collectors. The point collectors will also want to know what level you are on (56's 28's or 21's) which examiner you had and what points you dropped. The schools then compile the data collected by the point collectors and then they send a list of all the questions from all of the appearances for that day by email to everybody that has paid a subscription fee to the school. These sheets are known as the daily sheets. The daily sheets are the questions you work through with your cop. The daily sheets cover all levels with 56's questions first at the top of the page followed by 28's and so on. When on 56's make sure you clear the daily sheet of all 56's questions everyday. When on 56's if you have cleared the sheet try a few 28's questions. When on 28's I recommend you do 21's questions as well as clearing the 28's questions if possible.

On 56's the examiners are expecting a reasonable line but on 28's they expect you to know your stuff so are looking for tighter lines. To improve your lines you will need to know about the moving string.

The moving string is an advanced point to point method. I will now attempt to explain it here. When you first string your line up as a beginner you tend to pen up your line as close to the string as possible without moving the string, this is called the static line. The string will normally tell you which bridge to cross, now since you have to cross this particular bridge your continuing journey must start from the other side of the bridge so you should now move the string from your original start point moving it from the bridge to your end point. You will now find your line has moved considerably and this now changes the run. So on long runs that go across the map you move the string at major junctions that the string is telling you to go through for example if you are going across the map from east to west the static string will tell you which bridge to cross but if it's obvious by the string that you must go through elephant and castle junction you string up from the start point to elephant and castle junction and then string up from elephant and castle junction to the end point and now you might find that your bridge has changed so you string up from the elephant and castle to your new bridge and then put your string from the other side of the bridge to the end point, then if the string is dictating that you go through Hyde Park corner you string up to Hyde Park corner and then move the string from Hyde Park corner to the end point and so on. This method takes a little bit of getting used to but once you get the hang of it it gives you the most direct route possible and improves your lines no end. The moving string is an absolute game changer and it is essential you are proficient with it by the time you get to 28's at the latest. When I was on the Knowledge there was an examiner (now retired) that used to ask long lines across the map. This examiner was a master at the moving string and knew exactly what they wanted. The key to understanding their runs was the moving string and you would never truly understand what the examiner wanted without employing the moving string for example the examiner wasn't happy if you went over the park when he wanted you to go under it! To know what he wanted put your string at the point where you enter the park and then put the string where you leave the park and the answer will be obvious!

Doing the Knowledge is a full time job. Every single day you will have to call over your blue book, revise your points, clear the daily sheet with your cop as well as go out on your bike looking at new points that come out on the sheets and checking on road restrictions and set downs you are not sure of or can't see properly. If you have a full time job so you are on the Knowledge part time your workload is no different than students who are fortunate enough to be able to study full time! So that means that if you are not working or sleeping you must study the Knowledge and when you are asleep you will be dreaming about it. The Knowledge becomes your whole life. You will have no time for holidays, friends, socialising, hobbies, nothing at all but the Knowledge, as a guide if the Knowledge hasn't completely overtaken your life you are not doing it properly. If you are a family person it will be very tough for your partner and children as well as yourself.

A WORD OF WARNING: You cannot do the Knowledge from a computer; you must go out and see points, road layouts, junctions etc. for yourself. Examiners are extremely experienced people they have thousands of people calling over in front of them, they can tell by the way you call over, which blue books/ Knowledge school you are using, how much work you have done, how hard you are working, what your weaknesses are, what your strengths are, how much more harder you need to work and they absolutely hate it if they can see you have been doing the Knowledge from a computer instead of a bike. They have plenty of tricks and tools in their armoury to confirm their suspicions and if they think you have been doing the Knowledge from a computer you will be absolutely caned and kept on the Knowledge longer than is necessary so don't do it. Don't get me wrong the computer has it's place, to help me memorize points I used to do a little bit of research on them which helped me to not forget them. I will give an interesting example of how I used to memorize some points. One day Berry Bros and Rudd St James's Street came out on the daily sheet so I went to see it on my bike. After I had pointed it I thought to myself that it looked an interesting point so I decided to Google it hoping to find something of interest that would make the point stick. After Googling it I found out that they had the most Masters of Wine in the world (six). This prompted the question what is a Master of wine? I discovered that to be a Master of Wine is very similar to doing the Knowledge you have to do years of self study learning absolutely everything about wine and wine tasting. You need to know all the vineyards of the world as well as every wine. There is a 70% failure rate on the exams. A Master of Wine can taste a wine and not only tell you what it is but they can tell which vineyard it came from. The next question I had was where do you go to be a Master of Wine? You need to go to The Institute of Masters of Wine Kirtling Street Battersea. Knowledge students will already know Nine Elms Lane, Cringle St R Kirtling St for the Riverlight Appartments, The Institute of Masters of Wine is in the same block as Sainsburys. So now I will never forget Berry Bros and Rudd St James's St but I also now know the point the Institute of Masters of Wine and I am also reminded of Riverlight Appartments Kirtling Street.

Going back to point to point if you have just started point to point and are struggling with it take heart from my experience. It took me two years to do my blue books and points properly. Then as soon as I had finished my blue books I joined a call over club and my first ever call over session was with a guy on 28's. He was absolutely mustard and was calling fluent lines bang on the string with no hesitation whatsoever so I immediately saw the standard that's needed. When it was my turn to call I couldn't see a line at all. I wasn't able to call a line. On point to point the worst thing you can call is an illegal (Banned turn or no entry etc) or a banana (very wide line). Well I couldn't even call a banana and this guy was smashing out perfect lines on the string. I went away from the call over club very despondent. Because of my army training giving up was never ever an option but on this occasion after studying so hard for two years and doing everything properly to find I couldn't call a line at all for the first time on the Knowledge I began to think maybe this is not for me. It was one of my lowest points on the Knowledge but I quickly snapped out of it and started penning up runs as soon as I got home I then started calling runs into a Dictaphone and didn't stop until I could at least call a banana. The problem with my bananas were that they were called bananas not because of the shape like everybody else's but mine were so far out that they were closer to South America where they grow bananas than South Kensington. Practice makes perfect I just kept calling runs and penning them up and gradually I was able to call an acceptable line and eventually over time I got as good as the guy I met at the call over club. When I got onto 28's I had some luck and managed to find a call over partner that was on 21's that was also full time. My new cop was a master of the moving string and he was a real game changer for me. We worked extremely hard, him because he was close to getting out (Knowledge speak for finishing the Knowledge) and me because I knew he would get out soon and I would lose him as a call over partner and would have to find another one. So the moral of this story is no matter how bad you think you are at point to point if you keep at it it will definitely come.

Chapter Nine

The Hippocampus

The Knowledge of London is a unique system in many ways. It was discovered at University College London that London Black cab drivers have a larger brain than anybody else. The hippocampus part of the brain that is responsible for navigation grows physically bigger for a London black cab driver. University College also tested their own medical students but their hippocampus was the same size as everybody else so they thought it might be something to do with driving so they tested bus drivers but again bus drivers had the same size hippocampus as everybody else. They then tested retired cabbies that had stopped working and discovered their hippocampus had gone back down to normal size so to conclude your hippocampus is used while you are thinking and calculating a line or route in your mind. Calculating a complicated route across London with all the one way streets and systems is a complicated puzzle in itself; we are the only people that can do it without looking at a map and what's more is we have to do it in seconds.

The reason I include this chapter in the book is because it's important and helpful for a new student to be aware that your brain is like a muscle and although you may think that you don't have the memory to do the Knowledge you absolutely do you will just have to train your brain just as you would your body in the gym if you wanted to get fitter.

Straight after I did my first run Manor House Station to Gibson Square I couldn't remember it. To help me remember it I had to write it down and then draw a little word association cartoon next to each road name to help me remember. It took me two or three days to remember the first run. Then I managed to get the next few runs down to a day to remember them then it was just a morning or afternoon to remember a run. After about thirty runs I found I could stop drawing the cartoons. Then I could remember a run in just a couple of hours, then it was an hour and after a while I could remember longer runs in just ten minutes and then came that magical day when one day I was riding back home down the motorway when I found I could remember and call the days run before I got home and didn't need to take any notes or try to remember it. So remembering and calling a run had gone from two or three days to instantly! This demonstrates that your brain is truly a muscle and your brain can be trained and developed just like any other part of your body.

Speaking of the brain in 2008 my wife and I had a daughter who was born with autism. Anybody that has had an autistic child will tell you that you go from knowing nothing or little about autism to becoming an expert. You become an expert because you study the subject as much as you can to help your child. In fact one of the many reasons I became a London black cab driver was so that I had the flexibility with my work to be able to work around and help our daughter. By studying my daughter I learnt many things about myself. We all have these autistic traits but some people have them more than others. I have autistic traits but not enough to put me on the spectrum or give me a diagnosis. The positive autistic traits I have are that I am extremely focused and if I choose a subject to study I study it intensely to expert level, obviously this is an asset when studying something like the Knowledge. I have noticed that some London black taxi drivers have high functioning autism. The job is attractive to high functioning autistic people because not only do they like to study the Knowledge but the job also allows them to work relatively solitary and do as they please which is very important to somebody on the spectrum. I'm sure there's a link somewhere so I hope one day the researchers that discovered the hippocampus changes in London black taxi drivers are able to find something that can help with autism. You read it here first.

Chapter Ten

Appearances

Why is an appearance called an appearance? Well on the Knowledge with the exception of point to point the Knowledge is all self study and the examiners never see you until you *appear* in front of them. Secondly an appearance is many things, it's an examination of your topography knowledge, it's a job interview, it's an inspection of your turn out and it's a test of character and a test of temperament so covering all of these things it needs its own name you cannot just call it an examination or a job interview because it is all of these things and more.

When I was doing my blue book runs I used to hear people say how frightening and scary appearances were. I used to think to myself look; it's just two people in a room having a chat get a grip and man up. I used to think to myself there is no way appearances are going to intimidate me because firstly I'm a confident person, job interviews have never bothered me, I've been in the army and had Regimental Sergeant Majors and Provost Sergeants shouting at me just one inch from my face, I've had people try and kidnap me in South America when I was unarmed with no back up and am alive to tell the tale so I will be fine.

HOW WRONG WAS I!!!!!!!! I found appearances the most unpleasant thing in my whole life and completely melted in every one of them!

I am trained in fear control so I thought it would come in handy for appearances but in reality it worked against me. Back when we were cavemen we had to face danger everyday fighting wild animals etc. so when we used to get an adrenalin rush we used to be very familiar with it, recognise it, harness it, control it, and use it to our advantage in the way of fight or flight in other words we would either stay and use up the adrenalin to fight the wild animal or use up the adrenalin running away. Now in modern life we don't often meet wild animals we have to fight so when we do face danger we get an unpleasant feeling in the way of an adrenalin rush and often mistake this for fear and freeze but if we are trained to recognise it we learn how to control it and use it in our favour.

Going into an appearance as I was being called into the office by the examiner I would feel the adrenalin rush recognise it and automatically welcome it into my system as I had been trained however as I was neither going to fight a knowledge examiner (Not recommended) or going to immediately sprint to Charing Cross Station I was sitting in the appearance chair with a body full of unused adrenalin and if you don't use it up you will melt into a quivering wreck and that's what happened to me every time. Out of 24 appearances there was only one where I was happy with what I called over.

The first thing you should concentrate on an appearance is your turnout. Less experienced people greatly underestimate the interview side of the Knowledge, some people even go through the whole process thinking they are only being tested on their topography knowledge. You should attend every appearance suited and booted. You should dress as you would for your wedding day unless you are female of course I don't recommend turning up in your wedding dress! Some people think because they have a suit on they are smart, wearing the same old crumpled suit that you wear to work everyday is not smart. I used to go the extra mile with my turn out for my appearances so much so that I was complimented on my turn out by three different examiners on three separate appearances. Remember you only have one chance to make a first impression. On the Knowledge you see several different examiners, I had them all so potentially you need to dress to make that first impression on every appearance in case you see an examiner you have never seen before. First of all I bought a brand new suit, shirt and tie that I would only wear on appearances. I would make sure my shoes were polished to army parade ground standard. I would have a short neat army issue haircut before every appearance and then employ an old army trick we used to do before an important parade was to shave as close as possible as late as possible before going to bed, this has two purposes firstly when you shave first thing the following morning most of the work has been done and you seem to be able to get even closer but more importantly if for any reason your alarm clock doesn't go off and you find yourself rushing to get to the train station and there is no time to shave it's damage limitation, at best nobody will notice you haven't shaved and at worse it won't look as bad as if you hadn't had a close shave the night before. Incidentally you have to turn up suited and booted every time you go to the Carriage Office while you are on the Knowledge. When I was on my voluntary map test three candidates didn't bother and the examiner didn't say anything so I was thinking to myself that I needn't have bothered making the effort to go suited and booted and then at the end before we all left the examiner pointed the three out and asked them to stay behind!

When you turn up for appearances you have an appointment card with a time on it, this time is not the time of your appearance but the time you should report to the reception desk and book in. After booking in the receptionist will send you through to the waiting room. The waiting room is like a dentists waiting room with other candidates already waiting like lambs to the slaughter. The waiting room has an intimidating silence to it, you can feel the tension in the atmosphere, just sitting in the waiting room is terrifying and all of this is cleverly designed to test your character it really is an experience that you cannot explain unless you have done it. To add to the fear factor one particularly tough examiner would come out of their office as if to call somebody's name and everybody would be filled with dread and immediately look at the floor, this is what soldiers do on parade when the troop sergeant asks for volunteers to work the weekend, soldiers on parade always think that if they look down they become invisible or vanish into thin air. The examiner would look around the waiting room and then disappear back into their office and everybody would sigh with relief as if they had dodged a bullet. When a tough examiner came out and called somebody else's name all of the other candidates would selfishly think that's good if the examiner is occupied with them I might be called in by an easier examiner that likes to ask banker runs. Banker runs are an examiners favourite points and runs that they like to repeat over long periods of time which means they will come out often on the daily sheets so if you are doing the sheets properly and clearing them everyday you will know these runs by heart so in theory at least you should be able to call them well, have a relatively easy appearance and score (pass that appearance).

Your First Appearance

After the examiner has called your name you follow them from the waiting room back to their office. The first thing the examiner will ask you is for your scorecard. The examiners like to see a clean uncreased scorecard. I had learnt this from doing my research before I started the Knowledge so I invested in a hard case cover especially for my scorecard, some students use plastic bags and of course the students that don't bother to polish their shoes and can't work out why they are not scoring on appearances don't use anything. Now imagine you are an examiner and you have two candidates to see for their first appearances. You have never met or seen either of them before in your life. All you have to go on before you see them are your notes. Candidate "A" according to his file says he took his full two years studying his blue books. He attended the voluntary map test and scored 92% on his map test. Candidate "B" only took 18 months studying his blue books, he didn't bother doing the voluntary map test and just scraped through his map test with 62%. Who do you think the examiner will think needs testing the most? The Knowledge is all about giving yourself the best chance. Don't be Candidate "B".

On your first appearance the examiners are supposed to go "easy" on you only asking big points like train stations or large hotels etc. and the runs are supposed to be based on the blue book runs. At this point on your Knowledge journey you should know your blue book inside out so it may sound easy but you will be surprised how easy it is for the examiners to "disguise" a blue book run by just moving the beginning and end points or asking the run backwards or lengthening or shortening it slightly or any combination of the things I have just said. To give you examples and demonstrate some runs based on the blue book I will list some here See if you can recognise them and I will give the answers at the end of this chapter.

Lambs Conduit Street to Offord Road

New Cross Station to Royal observatory

Dr Johnsons Avenue to Putney Hill

Walworth Police Station to Snow Hill Police Station

Olympia to Putney Bridge

Eastmans Dental College to Bakers Lane

Townmead Road to Print Works

Cloudseley Square to Christina Square

Stamford Hill to Oxo Tower

Tite Street to Hong Kong City Restaurant

Wandsworth Bridge to Ronnie Scotts Club

Farringdon Station to Manor House Station

I will now come onto the appearance scoring system. The appearance scoring system is quite complicated, when you are on the Knowledge and are on appearances you get into the swing of things quick enough but to a layman it's always tricky trying to explain it so for the purposes of this book I will slightly simplify it. Basically on an appearance you either score (pass) or you don't (fail). Remember you can't fail the Knowledge you can only give up. But you can fail the map test or any number of appearances. The first level of appearances you are tested every 56 days to get onto the next level (28's) you have to get the best of seven, that is to say you need to score four times. After you have scored four times out of seven you then have to appear every 28 days to get tested. If the examiners get the best of seven (you fail four times) you then get what is called "Red lined" and you go back to the beginning of that stage and you get a second go of trying to get the best of seven and onto 28's. If you don't get the best of seven on the second time around and get your "drop" to 28's you get red lined again and you go back to the previous stage in this case the map test. If you are successful and get your drop to 28's the same procedure starts again you need the best of seven to get onto 21's and then after the best of seven on 21's you get what's called your Requisition and have reached the required standard and have passed the Knowledge of London and the examiner puts his or her hand across the table and shakes your hand, up until this point it is forbidden to touch or shake an examiners hand. Although it's possible nobody usually goes back two stages so if you are on 21's you may get red lined back to 28"s but you are usually safe from getting red lined back to 56's and if you are on 28's you may get red lined back to 56's but you won't usually go back to the map test. You are under the most pressure on appearances when the score is 3-3 because it's all or nothing you either go through to the next stage or get red lined back to the beginning. Nobody wants to get red lined on 56's because of the obvious time delay but it's especially tough if you go back to 56's from 28's and I am told many students give up at that point, those that keep going after going from 28's to 56's are very determined individuals indeed. If you get red lined on 21's it's not the end of the world because appearances come around like lightning on 21's. I never really got used to appearances but on 21's by then you really know your stuff and appearances come around so fast you get kind of numb to them and you are usually so "battle worn" by then you just take what comes. When you do finally get your Req that feeling of achievement and elation is indescribable. For me it was more of a sense of relief. You have a strange mix of feeling on top of the world and relief that it's all over.

The answers to the disguised blue book runs are as follows:

Lambs Conduit Street to Offord Road   Run 2 Thornhill Square to Queen Square (Backwards)

New Cross Station to Royal observatory   Run 14 New Cross Station to Maritime Museum

Dr Johnsons Avenue to Putney Hill   Run 24   Manor Fields to Bedford Hill (Backwards)

Walworth Police Station to Snow Hill Police Station   Run 50 Lorrimore Square to Central Criminal Court

Olympia to Putney Bridge   Run 110 Lacy Road to Olympia (Backwards)

Eastmans Dental College to Bakers Lane   Run 118 York Way to North Hill (Extended)

Townmead Road to Print Works   Run 145 Redriff Road to Bagleys Lane (Backwards)

Cloudseley Square to Christina Square   Run 1 Manor House Station to Gibson Square (Backwards)

Stamford Hill to Oxo Tower   Run 153 Stamford Street to Stamford Hill (Backwards)

Tite Street to Hong Kong City Restaurant   Run 274 Royal Hospital to Ilderton Road

Wandsworth Bridge to Ronnie Scotts Club   Run 272 Townmead Road to Old Compton Street

Farringdon Station to Manor House Station   Run 199 Lordship Road to Farringdon Station (Backwards)

These blue book runs have only been disguised very slightly by just moving the points and in some cases asking the run backwards. Hopefully you will see from this that learning your blue book backwards is very worthwhile. Many students say that there's no need to bother because you will learn them backwards anyway with the hours and hours spent on the map doing point to point and indeed this is very true as eventually on 21's and Req standard you should be able to be asked anything anywhere but learning them backwards early will make this less of a struggle and you will know your blue books so well forwards at map test stage that you are more tweaking what you already know than fresh learning so the reward to effort ratio is extremely high what's more you will now have 640 blue book runs instead of 320!

After you have finished your appearance the examiner will return your scorecard so you will know immediately if you have scored or not. When you score on appearances it's a great feeling and obviously a no score is disappointing. Everybody has their fair share of not scoring on appearances and you are expected to take a no score on the chin taken with good grace Knowledge examiners hate bad losers. On the Knowledge it can feel like you are working really hard but examiners can see that you should be working a lot harder even if you can't see it yourself. So if you are not scoring on appearances dust yourself down and be honest with yourself if your study system is not working you need to change something, with so much to cover everyday you can't do it all so your study becomes a balancing act giving priority to your weaknesses but still trying to fit in everything else around it, maybe you are not calling your blue book enough, once you know your blue book inside out many students drop it in the later stages, this is a mistake because it is important to keep calling it for fluency. Calling your blue book every day helps you to call your point to point and appearance runs fluently without hesitation. Or maybe you are not scoring because you are doing too much map work and not enough bike work or vice versa, the examiners will know your weaknesses and will tell you so make sure you listen to the examiners advice because they will be writing in their notes what your weaknesses are and what advice was given and they will be checking on later appearances to see if you have listened to them and taken their advice.

After you have left the examiners office hopefully with a nice score on your scorecard you report back to reception and then the person on the desk will give you another appointment for 56 days time or 28 days time or 21 days time depending what level you are on.

When you leave the building the points collectors from the Knowledge schools will be waiting for you to go over to them and give them the details of your appearance. Always give your runs in to the points collectors because these are what make up the daily sheets of which examiner is currently asking which points and what runs. The daily sheets are the lifeblood of people on appearances. I always handed in my runs to the points collectors on every single one of my appearances some students that didn't score wouldn't hand in their points to the points collectors for reasons best known to themselves these people were very selfish bad losers. The Knowledge will always reveal your true character at different stages of the process.

If for any genuine reason you can't hand in your points to the points collectors for example you are cutting it fine with a train you need to catch or sometimes the points collectors are simply not there for one reason or another all the schools have email addresses and online forums you can send your appearance points and runs to.

Whenever I was on an appearance I would always start to feel relief when I was calling the third run, I would think to myself this is nearly over. And then when I had set down the fourth run I would always feel very relieved the appearance was over and whatever happened I wouldn't need to do this again for another fifty six days. Then I would get more and more anxious as it got closer and closer to my next appearance. When I went to the supermarket and bought milk I would start feeling anxious if I noticed the "sell by" date on the milk was very close to my appearance date. You really can't know what an appearance is like unless you've done one.

Chapter Eleven

Meet the Examiners

If you think I am going to write gossip about examiners from the Knowledge grapevine I'm afraid you are going to be very disappointed. I have nothing but respect for all of the examiners. I had 24 appearances including my finals and had all of the examiners except one although the examiner I didn't have I had on my voluntary map test. I learnt something from all of the examiners especially the one I didn't score with and I probably learnt more about the Knowledge and about myself with the examiners that did score me on the appearances I had with them where I wasn't scored if that makes sense.

Good Cop Bad Cop

Remember it was the London Metropolitan Police that were in charge of the Carriage Office, were responsible for the Knowledge and took all appearances.

Way back in the day when there was no technology or forensics all the police could do was interview, question or interrogate people, or as they would prefer to call it "Taking a statement". After many thousands of hours taking statements they obviously got very good at it. They discovered when questioning people that generally everybody seemed to fit into one of two categories.

The first type of person if you shouted at him bullied him and generally tried to intimidate him he would tell you anything you wanted to know. And if you tried to be nice and reasonable with him he would see this as a weakness on your part and tell you nothing.

Conversely if you applied the same tactics of shouting, bullying and aggression to the second category of person you would get their back up and they wouldn't tell you anything at all but if you were nice to them and civil to them they would try and help you as much as they could.

So when interviewing a new suspect they had to find out which of the two categories the suspect fell into as quickly as possible. The police found the quickest way to find this out was to employ both methods. Firstly a policeman would enter the room taking the "bad cop" role being very loud, shouty and aggressive. Then after the "Bad Cop" had left the room the "Good Cop" would enter all calm and friendly pretending to like the suspect perhaps offering a cigarette or a brew and even pretending not to like the bad cop himself, saying something along the lines of "Don't take any notice of my colleague he's just an arsehole" They would then find out which cop was getting the results they were looking for and carry on with the relevant tactics.

So when the police started to take appearances on the Knowledge with the remit of testing character as well as an exam it was only natural for them to bring their "Good Cop" "Bad Cop" techniques across to the Knowledge.

On the Knowledge there is a good mixture of examiners male and female, varying ages, "good cops"," bad cops" and middle of the road firm but fair examiners. They are supposed to represent the mixed bag of customers you will get in the cab. I will not name any individual examiners because although they usually stay for a long period of time they do change over time.

Every generation of examiners have their "Arch Villain" an examiner with a very tough reputation capable of making an advanced student feel like they don't know anything and filling all students with dread. This tradition is so ingrained into the Knowledge that I met at least three very old time cabbies from three completely different generations who all thought that the fictional character nicknamed "The Vampire" in Jack Rosenthal's 1979 film "The Knowledge" was based on an examiner from their time on the Knowledge!

The stories of examiners testing candidate's characters on appearances before political correctness have gone down into folklore. Some of them include allowing a student to "choose" his first point of a run by blindfolding him and making him throw a dart at the map. An old cabbie I know said that the examiner pulled down the blinds with the office lights off and the whole appearance was conducted in the pitch black. Another examiner had a wooden model of a parrot on his windowsill behind him and he would position the candidate's chair so that the parrot looked like he was sitting on the examiners shoulder just like "Long John Silver" the fictional pirate in "Treasure Island". Other examiners liked to distract the candidates by dropping or snapping pens and pencils or taking a personal telephone conversation in the middle of an appearance. Some examiners liked to give runs that could be taken as an insult for example a candidate with a slight petty criminal record might be asked Pentonville Prison to the Rehabilitation Centre or a candidate that had revealed they were doing the Knowledge because they had lost their job might be asked the point of where they worked to the Job Centre. The stories are endless. This type of strange behaviour was supposed to simulate the strange things that can happen in the cab and when they do happen you still have to think of your line whether you are in an appearance or a cab. On appearances the examiners want to see how you are going to deal with these situations.

Today now we are more politically correct the character tests on the Knowledge by modern examiners are not so extreme as in the past but they are still there but a bit more subtle.

When being called into the examiners office I have heard of examiners running into their offices quickly so the candidate is not sure which office he is in and then the examiner starts asking points while the candidate is still outside or just entering the office. One of my call over partners said the examiner pretended to get his name wrong when calling him in for his appearance and then when the appearance started the examiner pretended to be deaf. This type of pantomime is not as silly as it sounds you really do get all of these situations and a lot worse in the cab so the examiners want to know and see how you are going to deal with it.

Customers in the cab can be very nice or they can be a bit impatient or they may be sarcastic or downright rude and all at no fault of your own and appearances are trying to simulate all of this. Just like in a cab you don't know what customer you will get next, on appearances you don't know which examiner you are going to get next.

When you enter the examiners office say good morning/afternoon

Sir/Maam and then wait to be invited to sit down before you sit. The examiner will then ask you your first point to start the run. If you know the point give the address you are only required to give the street or road you do not need to give the number of the building. If you don't know the point the examiner will ask you another point near to the one you have just dropped. Each run starts off with ten points and then one point is deducted for each point you drop. After you have "pulled" (Knowledge speak for knowing where a point is) the first point the examiner will ask you the end point of the run and the same procedure happens again until you have pulled both the beginning and end points of the run successfully. You then think of your line before calling. While you are thinking of your line all examiners are different, some allow you as much time as you like within reason because they like to hear the best line you can come up with, other examiners will give you a reasonable amount of seconds and then hurry you up to start calling (Pulling away in your cab) and there is at least one examiner that likes you to start calling the run almost immediately this is because this is the most realistic when you are in the cab, customers expect you to leave immediately they don't expect you to just sit in your cab thinking of a line they want you to just get going. An examiner that wants you to leave immediately is usually known as a tough examiner because you are under a lot of pressure to leave but again the examiner only wants to see how you are going to handle the pressure when a customer jumps in the cab, gives you an address and says "GO!!!"

When you have thought of your line start calling confidently as if it's the best line in the world. Examiners are always looking for confidence above everything else. You will usually score better calling a line confidently without hesitation that's a bit wide than calling a tighter line with lots of stops and starts and hesitation. After you have called your run the examiner will deduct points at their discretion for hesitation and/or a wide route. You are asked four runs on every appearance with the exception of your finals (Suburb runs) where you are asked six.

The points and runs examiners ask are at their own discretion and each examiner has their own style. I will describe some of the examiners different styles when I was on the Knowledge although I won't name them out of respect for them and their privacy they will be recognisable to students on the Knowledge. The examiners all have their good cop/bad cop role but all examiners are capable of switching roles if it is needed. Some students believe because they have had a particular tough examiner they won't get them again on the next appearance, although the Carriage Office tries very hard to give you a mixed bag of examiners they are contrary to what some may believe only human and can go off sick or take an unexpected holiday for whatever reason and it can work out that you get the same examiner twice in a row, yet another reason to keep on your toes on the Knowledge. But take heart if they think they have already tested your Character enough and only a bad cop examiner is available for you a bad cop examiner is capable of being a good cop and throwing you a lifeline if they think it is relevant at this precise stage, likewise if they don't think your points knowledge has been tested enough a normally good cop /friendly examiner can absolutely smash you on points you've never heard of, so keep studying hard and stay on your toes. In fact on the Knowledge another thing that makes it so tough is that you need to permanently be on your toes, the examiners will push you to the limit and make sure you are working really hard at all times.

So here are a few of the examiners that tested me, the list is not complete.

One examiner used to virtually only ask banker runs, this examiner would ask the same points from his bank of points and ask long runs across the map. The examiners runs were long on 56's getting more detailed on 28's and even longer on 21's. The examiner was an absolute master of the moving string and new exactly what they wanted from the candidates. Because the examiner would ask from the same bank of points a hard working student wouldn't usually drop any points with this examiner but their runs needed to be spot on. If a candidate dropped points with this examiner it revealed that they weren't doing the daily sheets. Knowing what I now know if I had my Knowledge time over again I would have studied this examiners long 21 lines on 56's. A really good examiner unfortunately for Knowledge students now retired.

Another examiner that liked to call his own banker runs would ask very short easy runs but they would really teach you something useful, maybe a shortcut that cut off a junction with traffic lights or maybe a short cut that got around a banned turn, which is what the Knowledge is all about. This examiner would make sure you went out on your bike and did your quarter miles properly because with this examiner although it was relatively easy learning the runs the examiner knew every single point in the quarter mile areas that they asked. So obviously a good tactic for students was to go to the areas this examiner asked and make sure you pay special attention and pick up all the points in these areas. One of the areas this examiner likes to ask points from is Greenwich. Now bearing in mind that you shouldn't take days off from the Knowledge when you are studying the Knowledge one day my wife said to me it's a lovely day can't we just have one day off from the Knowledge and go out somewhere? My wife has many strong points but luckily geography is not one of them so I said sure I know this nice little village that has a market, we can start off by parking in the Royal Observatory walk down to the market through the nice gardens, visit the Cutty Sark and the Market, we can then explore the streets looking for a nice restaurant for a spot of lunch and then if there's time we can even walk through a foot tunnel and visit a city farm. Perfect she says, we genuinely had a good day out and without her knowing I pointed most of Greenwich. You have to use your head on the Knowledge. Whenever my wife asked me to cut the grass or paint the fence or something I would always say, "Don't worry, I will do it, I like to do it in my own time there's no need to keep nagging me every six months!"

Another examiner was also known as a points examiner. This examiner had a true photographic memory and knew all of the history and facts behind all of the points. The examiner used to interview you and then if in the mood was capable of pulling points and giving you points that connected to your name and all the facts, places and information that you had given. This examiner didn't seem to me to be too bothered about the line but if they thought you needed to be tested on your points they would "Smash" you on points that is to say continually ask you points that you are never going to pull until there were so many points deducted from the run for dropped points that there was nothing left to score with. In my case knowing that I live in Kent I was asked road after road in a dead end cul de sac in Harlesden. I always smiled and took my no score appearances with good grace knowing it was all part of the journeys swings and roundabouts.

Another examiner known as a tough examiner used to like asking the most obscure points that they could find, what's more they would make sure there were restrictions in the run, banned turns and one way streets etc. because on the Knowledge the rules are that if you call an illegal you score zero for that run. Here's a piece of advice for current students, if you know you have called an illegal don't go to pieces and give up the appearance I called an illegal on two different appearances and still scored on those appearances so an appearance isn't over until it's over. This examiner would also like to test your character by coming across as very abrupt and rude but with my life experience I am also a good judge of character and I can tell you that this examiner like all the other examiners is actually a nice person. Another rule on the Knowledge is that an examiner can ask a point up to six years after the point has gone e.g. a restaurant has closed or a building has changed or been demolished. Inexperienced students whinge about this rule but think about it, a tourist comes to London goes to a restaurant and enjoys the experience, the same tourist comes back to London in three years time or more and the restaurant has now closed. The tourist doesn't know the restaurant has closed so jumps into a cab and asks to be taken there, this actually happens in the cab so we need to train for it. Another thing that happens a hell of a lot in the cab is a foreigner pronouncing places so bad that it can take a while to understand where they actually want to go. One of my call over partners said that on one of his appearances the examiner asked French Restaurants in a French accent for the whole appearance.

When I am out in the cab and get asked points, roads, and places by customers I often smile to myself and immediately think of the particular examiners that like to ask these points on appearances. Just like on the Knowledge it's satisfying to see one of your own points you chose to point come out on the daily sheet or better still be asked by an examiner on an appearance it's satisfying to be asked by a customer a point that you had to answer on an appearance.

After completing the Knowledge I am extremely impressed with the process. Whenever I play Chess I always admire whoever originally thought of the game and then how it evolved over time into genius, football fans must think the same

about the game and rules of football.

Final thoughts on the Knowledge

If I were asked what should be changed on the Knowledge my honest answer would be absolutely nothing. Some students say the red line rule should go but these are usually students that haven't worked hard enough, of course they think they are working hard, getting up at 4a.m going out on the bike in freezing weather, calling over runs, collecting and revising points etc. but the hard truth is the Knowledge can be a brutal sport and you may think you are working hard but I'm afraid it's not hard enough. Nobody said it was going to be easy. I went to 3-3 on 56's before getting my drop to 28's and was then red lined once on 28's so I know what pressure feels like and I know what being red lined feels like. When I got red lined I smiled at the examiner, thanked them and took it on the chin. I smiled and showed kindness to the examiner because everybody thinks of the poor student getting red lined but nobody thinks that it's not a pleasant job for an examiner that has to red line somebody that has been working very hard. The red line is needed for the examiners to use as a tool for making you work harder and testing your grit and determination and to take that away would dilute the Knowledge and would be a big mistake in my opinion. I believe every decision the examiners made on my Knowledge journey was the correct one. Because the examiners do their job properly when you do finally get out and into your cab you are able to do the job with ease, you are among the most highly trained taxi drivers in the world. The Knowledge is truly one of the things that make Britain great; to dumb it down or disband it would be a genuine crime.

Knowledge speak

Appearance   A one to one oral examination with a Knowledge of London examiner. An appearance is an examination, a job interview and a turn out inspection and a test of character all rolled into one.

Badge day   The day shortly after your finals when you have finished the Knowledge of London and are presented with your Knowledge of London certificate and your new badge and bill.

Banana   A wide run so called because the line on the map when penned up looks like a banana

Bankers   Examiners favourite runs asked often or on a relatively regular basis

Bill   A London taxi drivers license to drive a London taxi anywhere in the whole of London

Blue book   A Knowledge student's book listing the 320 runs required to be learnt forwards and backwards by heart

Butter boy   A brand new driver recently passed the Knowledge

The Chair   The most terrifying thing to a Knowledge student; sitting in "The Chair" in an appearance.

COP   Call over partner. Somebody you practice with to call over runs and pen them up on the map

The drive   The advanced driving test

Drop   can be positive or negative. In the negative if you don't know a street or point you are said to "drop it" for example "The student was so nervous in front of the examiner he dropped The British Museum!" In the positive when you pass an appearance that puts you onto the next stage you are said to get your "Drop" for example "I hope to get my drop to 28's by Christmas" or after passing his appearance he got his drop to 21's"

Finals   After completing the Knowledge of London you have one final appearance based on the suburb runs and all the Heathrow airport terminals

The Handshake   After you have completed the Knowledge of London you are permitted to shake the examiners hand

Map test   The very first test on the Knowledge. This is the only test on the Knowledge where you will need a pen

On the string or cotton   A very direct route because the roads of the route follow the tightly pulled string between two points on the map

Per Cent   Knowledge students love to speak in percentages. When knowledge is passed on from student to student it is vital that it is correct and up to date because getting the wrong knowledge in your head can cost you or somebody else an appearance therefore there is a lot of responsibility giving knowledge so students need to be very honest of how sure they are about giving knowledge e.g. "I'm not sure if you can turn right into Stratton St, I'm 70% sure you can't". Or "100% you can't turn right into Stratton St I was there yesterday"

Point to point   The exercise Knowledge students do of thinking of a route between two points without looking at the map and then penning the line up on the map to see how close it is to the string

Point   Point of interest, train stations, hotels restaurants etc. Can be anything somebody gets in a cab and asks to go

Pull a point   To be able to remember and know where a point is whether asked by a Knowledge examiner, call over partner or a paying member of the public in your cab

Red lined   Being put back to the beginning of a stage or back to a previous stage after not scoring enough on appearances.

Req   Requisition reaching the required standard to be a London black taxi driver

Runs   Routes called by Knowledge students and London taxi drivers

See   To see a run or a point in your minds eye. E.g. a Knowledge teacher or cop may say, "Can you see the Landmark Hotel?"

Set Down   where you pullover or park up so a customer can get out

Smashed on points   When a Knowledge examiner asks a Knowledge student so many points the student doesn't know, that the student is unable to score

Spin   Another word some Knowledge students use for a turn around. For some reason I always hated this term and never used it and called a turn around a turn around.

The suburbs   The final runs you learn in preparation for your final Knowledge appearance

The talk   The introductory welcome talk given by the Carriage Office to new students on the Knowledge

Cabbie Slang

Be Lucky   A cabbies farewell to another cabbie due to the job relying so much on luck

Bilker   Somebody that takes a taxi ride and then runs off without paying.

Bill   Taxi driver's licence

Billy   from Cockney rhyming slang Billy Bunter= Punter or sometimes

Hillman   Hillman Hunter=Punter

Broom   To refuse a fare. If there is another taxi driver behind you, either on a rank or on the street you are said to broom back the job to the driver behind you. (Usually used in a negative sense)

Bull Ring   Royal Hospital entrance on Chelsea Embankment where cabbies rank for The Chelsea Flower Show

Burst   When all the people leave after a timed event, theatres, concerts and shows are all said to burst, e.g. "I'm finishing work and going straight home after the theatre burst"

Canary   A London cab driver only licensed to ply for hire in the suburbs called a canary because they have a yellow badge instead of the Green badge licensed to ply for hire anywhere in London

Clock   Taxi Meter   e.g. "I had a dozen quid on the clock" (I had twelve pounds on the meter)

A Churchill   A meal. So called because Winston Churchill brought in a law that said a cabbie didn't need to accept a fare while he was eating

Dead Zoo   The Natural History Museum

Dog   Negative word for a taxi driver that doesn't follow the etiquette especially picking up close to ranks and pulling out in front of other drivers or overtaking to get the next job

At the death   Last job of a shift, e.g. "I had a bad shift but managed to take a score at the death"   (I had a bad shift but managed to take twenty pounds at the very end of my shift)

Flag Fall   Minimum Fare set by the Carriage Office

Flyer   An airport job

Grafter   Driver who works long hard hours

Green Badge   An all London taxi driver

Hickory   Meter (From cockney rhyming slang; Hickory dickory dock) e.g. "I've been bilked but luckily I only had seven quid on the Hickory" (I've had a runner but luckily there was only seven pounds on the meter)

Interview   Used mainly by night workers with locked doors speaking to a customer at the window to gauge their level of alcohol and assess whether they are likely to be trouble or not before unlocking the doors and letting them in.

The Iron Lung   Free public toilet popular with cabbies on the corner of Regency Street. So called because you need iron lungs to breath in the air inside

Journeyman   A taxi driver who rents a cab rather than owns it himself

The Kipper or Kipper Season   The winter months after New Year when business is very slow. Also used in other cash trades by fairground showmen and market traders. Very old saying when kippers were cheap it was all that seasonal workers could afford to eat out of season. Some also say trade is as flat as a kipper.

Leather arse   Driver who works long hard hours

Legal   The legal fare. Paying the exact fare without tipping e.g. "The tight bastard legalled me"   (The gentleman paid the correct fare)

Loaded Rank   A taxi rank with taxis on it. Exact opposite to an empty rank

Love Job   Taking family and friends for free

Musher   Owner Driver

On Point   First taxi on a taxi rank

Punter   Paying customer

Put On   Join a taxi rank

Rank Up   Join a taxi rank

The Raft   The Gatwick Express rank at Victoria Station

Rest Rank   Where a Cabbie can take a break without plying for
hire

Roader   A fare that has a long distance

Set Down   pullover or park up so a customer can get out

Set Fare   A price between a cabbie and client negotiated off the
meter

Sherbet   Cab   (From cockney rhyming slang sherbet dab=cab)

Shit Cart   An old poorly maintained scruffy cab

To trap   Get a Fare e.g. "It was busy today I trapped as soon as I got into town" or "It wasn't that busy today I didn't trap until the end of my shift"

A Stop   When a taxi enforcement officer finds a fault on your taxi and issues a notice to take it off the road until the fault is repaired or put right

Wrong Un   A negative word used for cabbies and customers alike. For cabbies somebody that doesn't follow the etiquette see *dog*. And for customers somebody that doesn't pay see *bilker* or any member of the public that is trouble

Cabbie Slang Concerning Money

A Back Door   A score   (Cockney rhyming slang**)**

A Bag   A grand   (From cockney rhyming slang a bag of sand)

Bees Wax   Income Tax   (From Cockney rhyming slang)

Bin Lid   A quid   (Cockney rhyming slang)

Boracic   Skint   (from Cockney rhyming slang Boracic lint)

A Bottle Two hundred pounds (from cockney rhyming slang bottle of glue)

A Box Six hundred pounds (From cockney rhyming slang box of tricks)

A Bulls Eye Fifty pounds (from the bulls eye on a dart board that scores fifty)

Butter and Lard Credit card (Cockney rhyming slang)

A Carpet Three hundred pounds (prison slang; you got a carpet in your cell after you had served over three years. The slang crossed over to cash paid traders)

Cockle A tenner (From cockney rhyming slang cock and hen)

A Jacks   A five pound note   (from cockney rhyming
slang Jacks

alive)

A Jockey   A tip   (From cockney rhyming slang Jockey Whip)

A Lady   A fiver   (From Cockney rhyming slang Lady Godiva)

A Monkey   Five hundred pounds

A Neves   Seven hundred pounds (Pronounced Nevis from
back slang)

A Oner   one hundred pounds (pronounced wunner)

Pie and Mash   Cash (Cockney rhyming slang)

A Pony   Twenty five pounds

A Ruof   Four hundred pounds (pronounced Roaf from back
slang)

A Score   Twenty pounds

Useful Contacts

www.taxitradepromotions.co.uk

www.wizann.co.uk

www.thelondonknowledgeschool.co.uk

BKS Beginner Knowledge School
Congreve Hall Tatum St SE17

About the author

This is the bit where it would normally say Andy Cabman is happily married and has three children and lives in Kent with his wife and daughter. Although this is true I like to go the extra mile so as a bonus I am throwing in some of my army memoirs to let the reader know where my never give up character came from to do the Knowledge. I hope it will inspire people that think they are weak to understand that if you put yourself in at the deep end and you can stand the heat of the kitchen you can do or overcome anything.

I should point out if you are interested in reading my army memoirs that there was no political correctness in the British army in the 1970's/80's and it was a pretty brutal place to be so if you are easily offended by bad language, black humour and general thuggish behaviour it's probably best that you don't read it.

Army Memoirs

One Man's Journey

By Andy Cabman

Army Memoirs

One Man's Journey

By Andy Cabman

Chapter one

School Years

I was born in 1963 and like the vast majority of people I am pleased to say I was born good. I grew up on a council estate in Kent. I was born with a gentle nature and quickly learnt that bad people saw this as weak and I became prey to bullies. I came from a good honest working class family and had good friends so despite being prey to bullies I had a happy childhood.

In my teens at secondary school I hated sport. Our school played football and rugby on alternate weeks. Every lesson the games teacher would pick out the two "Super Star" players of the combined classes to be team captains. The two team captains would then take it in turns to pick their teams obviously picking the players in order of quality. At the end you would always end up with one overweight pupil with glasses, one asthmatic pupil with two left feet and then lastly you had...........me.

Once the games teacher blew the whistle and the game started I would spend the time trying to stay as far away from the ball as possible and because I wasn't participating the time dragged on forever, the fact we weren't allowed to wear watches on the pitch only added to the torture, every time the games teacher finally blew the whistle signalling the end of the game after what felt like two lifetimes it was the most beautiful sound to me as it meant the game was over and I could go back indoors and put some more sensible clothes on.

Sometime in the penultimate year at school in the games lesson we had boxing. This was the only boxing lesson we ever had so it must have been on the school curriculum and the games teacher did it once just to cover the curriculum. I was matched with a pupil who was even weaker than I was because I beat him and gave him a nosebleed. I found that I didn't mind boxing because it was all down to me. I wasn't a team player because I hated relying on other people so a sport I could do where I was the only person in the team suited me down to the ground and I had heard that in sport if you don't come first and you come second that second place is a very high ranking you usually get silver or something so here was a sport where I could come second every time!

Around this time I started doing Kyokushinkai Karate once a week in a church hall. I didn't get very far with it or do it for long because unbeknown to me destiny was going to stop my karate training by me going in the army. I never set out to be a hard man I just wanted to make sure I wasn't going to be prey to life's bad people. I decided that it looked like if I didn't take action I was either going to be the hammer or the anvil and it turned out I was to choose the former.

Around 1978 a Captain and a Sergeant in full number two dress (best formal parade uniform) from the Army Careers Office came to our school to give a slide show presentation on a career in the army. I remember thinking to myself if you two pair of mugs think that I am going to fall for your bullshit army recruitment propaganda you must think I was born yesterday.

After watching lads skiing down snowy mountains, water Skiing in exotic places, dozing off in hammocks in the jungle and the food by the Army Catering Corpse making the banquet nights in the Ritz Hotel look like dog shit I was begging my two new best friends to sign me up immediately!

I duly went along to the Army Careers Office for a series of interviews and an army medical. The army medical consisted of a corporal from the Army Medical Corpse putting a stethoscope onto my chest just to check that I was alive and that was it. I accepted the Queen's shilling that had gone up to about £5 in 1978 and was also given army travel warrants and was told to report to the Army Selection Centre in Deepcut Surrey, a place I had never heard of. I was told that I would be there for two days.

Army Selection Centre

I boarded the very busy packed commuter train from my hometown in Kent one crisp autumn morning. The train was full of men in pin stripe suits and bowler hats with umbrellas and briefcases all reading a copy of the over sized Financial Times. I can still hear the distinct sound of all the train doors being slammed shut as the commuters sat down on the dust filled upholstered seats. I asked a commuter wearing a bowler hat if this was the train for Waterloo and he told me the train was going to Cannon Street another place I had never heard of in my life so I quickly jumped out of the train and waited for the next one.

On arriving at Deepcut there was an army NCO (Non commissioned Officer) again in full number two dress waiting for us on the platform of the train station. We then all piled into a white mini bus and headed off on the short journey to the Army Selection Centre. The Army Selection Centre was a bit like a stately home if I remember rightly, an impressive building with it's own grounds. We did loads of multi choice tick tests a bit like the Knowledge map test. I remember one of the questions was, "What weighs the most a ton of bricks or a ton of feathers?" I remember thinking to myself these F-ers are trying to trick me into the Infantry. We went on what we were told by an army Sergeant was a five mile run, I don't think that at this point in my life that I had been this distance before without at least two wheels underneath me. The run was through woods and along wooded canals. I remember feeling so out of breath I thought I was in need of an oxygen tent. I was one of the stragglers walking at the back because I was too tired to run anymore. The sleeping accommodation was clean and presentable. We were shown how to make a basic bed block (Neatly folded blankets and bedding into a perfect square). I had noted that the food was of an extremely low standard and for breakfast the milk on the cereals tasted like water. I was later to learn it tasted like water because it was water! In the army you get powdered milk in your rations that you mix with water. I also noted that with the cold beans that we were served we also had powdered eggs. Hiding behind the powdered eggs was a sausage filled with saw dust. I thought to myself this is probably just for the mugs on selection you must get the real nice food when you are in the proper regular army. Of course I was later to learn that the hardest test in the army is The Army Catering Corpse Test because nobody has ever passed it!

On the second day there was yet more tests and interviews. I had my final interview with a Captain in the Intelligence Corpse. I remember one of the questions he asked me was what type of home do I come from? "What's your home like?" At this time of my life I was just fifteen years old and slightly autistic so I took everything literally so I said a three bedroom council house. He must have thought to himself I've got a right thick twat here, fair play to him though he kept a straight face. He then asked me if I had a girlfriend (I did). I didn't think anything of it at the time, I didn't even think it was a strange question but obviously he was trying to suss out if I was gay or not (Being gay in the army of the 1970's was not permitted as they thought amongst other things it was a security risk being open to blackmail in the cold war). Then after more questions he finally said congratulations you've got a placement in JLR RCT (Junior Leaders Regiment Royal Corpse of Transport). I will never forget the very last words he said to me, "Make sure you get yourself fit before you go in, the army will get you fit anyway but it's better if you are already fit". I remember leaving the Selection Centre promising myself I was going to start training and get myself fit.

I was very close to my grandad my mum's dad. My grandad was a tough character an army boxer who served in WW2 he served in a couple of infantry regiments fighting hand to hand on the frontline. My granddad never spoke about the war. I remember as a child helping him have a clear out in the early 1970's we found his medals at the back of a drawer, he placed absolutely no personal value on them whatsoever in fact the ribbons were separate from the medals, on finding them he instantly gave them to me saying war is futile and a very bad thing. I was around nine or ten years old at the time. I took the medals home and my mum sewed the ribbons on for me telling me again that grandad and the others that made it back never spoke about the war. The medals were given to me at too young an age I got bored of them and swapped them for toys as kids do. I did manage to get a couple back at some stage but the others are gone forever.

The above story has always had an effect on me. Whenever I see veterans with their berets on and their medals I always think of my grandad and am suspicious of them, I know it's stupid because I personally know people that I have served with who have medals and fully deserve them and have every right to wear them with pride but I suppose everybody deals with war and grief differently. I was told that I would be there for two days.

In 1984 while serving in the regular army in Germany I got a message saying the Orderly Officer wanted to see me. I went down to the Officers Mess and found him. He said to me let's take a walk. He then gently informed me that my grandad had passed away. The army are usually brilliant when it comes to compassionate leave and they flew me straight out to the UK for my grandad's funeral. My grandad was a Chas and Dave fan so when I got back to Germany from the UK I blasted out Chas and Dave songs from our block for weeks after so to this day somewhere in the UK there's a load of Geordies, Jocks and Scousers Etc. that know a few Chas and Dave songs word for word!

After clearing out my grandad's stuff we found some army papers that I will reproduce here in his memory and to the many brave men that didn't make it home:

We have received an account of the gallant conduct of Corpl. James Scott while serving with the Sherwood Foresters on the Anzio beachhead.

"When the battalion was hard pressed during the fighting at the end of February, Corpl. Scott was wounded. He ignored his wound, and went on acting as runner between his platoon and company, traversing the shell-stormed ground time and again. He rendered first-aid to the wounded and saw that they got back. He took ammunition forward under fire- the small arms fire was particularly fierce at this time. On the following night he consented to go back to have his wounds treated after he had been given a direct order to do so. He was later promoted to lance-sergeant."

12.5.1944

My granddad never told us about the above when he was alive. We also found similar papers and accounts from a separate relative after their death and they also never mentioned it or spoke about it while they were alive. I think the vast majority of men that returned from war didn't see themselves as heroes but just men who found themselves born in the wrong place at the wrong time and just did their best and did what they had to do.

In the army it's traditional to counter sad shit with black humour so to lighten the mood I will tell an old army joke.

All the men are on parade and the Sergeant Major comes on parade and just shouts out at the top of his voice "SMITH!!!!! YOUR MUM'S DEAD"!!!!!!!!!!!!

Smith breaks down crying and sobbing

The next week the same thing all the men are on parade and the Sergeant Major comes on parade and just shouts out at the top of his voice "JONES!!!!! YOUR DAD'S DEAD"!!!!!!!!!!!!

Jones breaks down crying and sobbing

So the OC (Officer Commanding) takes the Sergeant Major to one side and says, "Sergeant Major I think you need to be a bit more tactful when breaking bad news of a bereavement to the men".

Sergeant Major replies, "Very good Sir!

The next week all the men are on parade and the Sergeant Major comes on parade and shouts out at the top of his voice:

"PARADE!!!!!!!!   PARAAAAAADE SHUN!!!!!!!!

ALL THOSE WITH A GRANDAD......ONE PACE STEP FORWARD...MARCH!!!!

WHERE ARE YOU GOING CABMAN"?!!!!!!!!!!!!!

Back to the story, so it's around 1979 I'm back from the Army Selection Centre, still at school but waiting to leave school and go into the army. I was around my grandads one day and he was explaining to me all of the different ranks of the army to me, I remember him telling me, "......an NCO with three stripes on his arm is a Sergeant and you may address him as Sergeant or Sarge............"

This explanation was to have consequences for me on the second day of my army training.

The warning from The Captain at The Army Selection Centre to get fit is ringing in my ears so I decide I will leave for school early each morning and run around the block near my house before school and build it up over the weeks. Day one I nearly collapse from exhaustion and as we would say in army slang bin it (Stop doing it). I decide to just go in the army as I am, after all the Captain did say if I weren't fit the army would get me fit anyway. This wasn't one of the best decisions I've ever made.

Chapter Two

Junior Leaders Regiment

The Junior Leaders Regiment RCT had been in Taunton Devon for years but I found myself one summers day at Azimghur Barracks Colerne near Bath Wiltshire as one of the first intakes of the recently moved Regiment. Azimghur Barracks was an old RAF airfield so it had lots of aircraft runways and aircraft hangers and was huge covering miles of open space all fenced off by high security fence of course. After being met at the train station by army personnel, loaded into white army buses and driven to what was to be our new home we all found ourselves in a spacious upstairs room to be processed. The room was above the cookhouse, which doubled up as a leisure centre and the NAFFI. The first thing we were given was a copy of the Official Secrets Act to read and sign. It made one of those software agreements the internet asks you to sign today short, basic and straightforward needless to say us scruffy bunch of sixteen year old civvies didn't bother with the reading part. We then formed an orderly queue and were issued with our army number. My army number started with 2454. We then went to the bedding store and were issued our bedding, two white sheets, two pillows, two pillow cases, two itchy brown blankets and a mattress so thin it was like one of those "Odour eaters" you put in your shoes. When everybody had got their bedding we all had to carry all of our own individual bedding which was very awkward and run with it to our new accommodation. Our troop had four rooms with ten steel beds in each room, a Troop Sergeant, a Troop Corporal and the Troop commander an officer with the rank of Lieutenant. The training staff showed us how to make bed blocks when we weren't sleeping in them and how to make a bed with "Hospital corners" when we were sleeping. We were told that we would never walk in a casual manner ever again on camp, in groups we would march everywhere in three ranks and if we went anywhere on our own we were still required to march properly. We then all got in three ranks outside and marched to a large aircraft hanger where all our kit was laid out for each individual recruit on ponchos with our name and numbers on them. There was a lot of kit, two pairs of black boots one for work and one for best, combat trousers, combat jacket, two combat shirts, lightweight trousers known as army denims, a boiler suit known as army fatigues, PT Kit, Steel helmet, 38 webbing (The training staff wore 58 webbing), number two dress, peaked "Twat hat", stable belt, mess tins, drinking mug, KFS (Knife fork, spoon), respirator (Gas mask) and much, much more. Again we had to gather it up in a kit bag, awkwardly gather up the rest and run with it back to the accommodation. Back at the accommodation we were taught how to wear the different items of uniform. We were given a lesson on ironing. Each room had an iron we had to share and take turns using but no ironing board. Instead of an ironing board the troop Sergeant showed us how to fold one of the brown itchy blankets into a square put it on the table each room had and iron our shirts and trousers so sharp you could cut your fingers on the creases. The sharp creases were achieved by spraying starch onto them (at our own expense) and then ironing the creases using plenty more starch. We were taught how to put puttees on; puttees were long brown itchy bandages that wrapped around the top of your boots and the bottom of your trousers. The army seemed to like everything itchy especially the shirts. The shirts were known as KF shirts and were so itchy that some people had an allergic reaction to them and had an official exemption certificate from the medical centre. The training staff asked us to put up our hand if we had started shaving. Two or three members of the troop put up their hand and then the training staff said you ALL shave now. We were not permitted to use electric razors and had to buy shaving foam. We were then taught how to "bull" (polish) our boots by making tiny circles with a yellow duster and polish. After bulling our boots they were like mirrors and you could see your face in them. Our boots were covered in dimples with just the heel and toe smooth. So we "only" had to bull the toes and the heels, the rest of the boot had to be highly polished including the soles! These were just our "working" boots; it was different for our "best" boots. Our best boots that we wore with our number two dress (Formal parade dress with peaked cap) had to be highly polished all over. Of course before you could polish them all over the dimples had to go. To get rid of the dimples you had to keep heating the end of a steel spoon in a candle flame and then run this over the leather to iron the dimples out then once the surface was smooth you could start bulling the whole of the boots all over. After I left the army I was determined to find a use for this skill in Civvie Street and I eventually found a use thirty five years later on the Knowledge appearances. The training NCO's had different boots to us, they had thicker soles on their boots with hob nail studs all over the heals and soles, these boots were called ammo boots and they would come into the block wearing a number two dress peaked cap nicknamed a "Twat hat" in army slang also carrying a pace stick (Stick used for drill) and they would slide all over the floors we had just polished.

Reveille was 6.30a.m sharp. We were awoken by an NCO smashing his pace stick on the steel bed frames, once awake he would not leave the room until everybody's feet were on the floor, "Hands off cocks on socks, get your f-kin feet on the floor!" We dressed shaved (for the first time for many of us) and marched over to the cookhouse for breakfast. As soon as we got back from the cookhouse we had to clean the living accommodation from top to bottom. Dust and polish everywhere with yellow dusters, clean all the glass windows, clean all the mirrors, toilets, showers, sinks, mop all of the floors and then put yellow polish on the floor and polish it to a shine with a bumper. A bumper was a big heavy metal block that had a hinged broom handle on it that was pushed up and down the corridors to give them a lovely shine so the training NCO's could come in and slide on the freshly polished floor in their ammo boots.

After the block had been cleaned we had to be stood by our beds ready to be inspected for the first time by the Troop Sergeant. The Troop Sergeant entered the room he was immaculately dressed in sharply creased barrack trousers and highly polished ammo boots. As it was summer he was in "shirt sleeve order" (Shirt sleeves rolled up above the elbow with highly starched, highly sharp creases). He was wearing a number two dress "twat" hat with the peak highly polished, closely shaven with a neat army regulation haircut. The three stripes on his green shirt were dazzling bright white and to complete the look of the terrifying drill sergeant that he was he had a pace stick under his arm. The bed blocks had to be so perfect and made with so much care that some recruits made them the night before and slept on the floor!

I was standing by my bed to attention and the troop Sergeant approached me.

He looked up and down with disgust at my immaculate kit and said, "This kit is in shit state!!!" "Do you want to be in this man's army Cabman!!!!!!!????

Me: "Yes Sarge"

He then looked at me as if I had just insulted every female member of his family and said: "Sarge?" "SAAARGE? Suasaaaaarge, Massaaaaarge or passaaaarge?"

"ONLY MY FRIENDS CALL ME SARGE!!!!!

AND CABMAN YOU ARE NOT MY FRIEND!!!!!!!!!!!!!

Me: "(Nervously) "Sorry Sergeant"

Troop Sergeant: (In soft gentle voice) "That's OK Cabman everybody's allowed to make one mistake."

Now with red face, eyes bulging and veins sticking out on his neck, moving to one inch from my face

"AND YOU'VE JUST MADE YOURS!!!!!!!!!!!!!"

What made the Junior Leaders Regiment one of the toughest and best regiments of the army at this time was all about time and our young age. Kids back then weren't as street wise as they are today, it was the fact we were only sixteen years old that made it so tough, we actually believed all the pantomime, we really did believe the Sergeant Major "Had it in for us", if we had been just that bit older the system wouldn't have worked so well. We would have had the experience to know it was all part of the game and the Sergeant Major most very likely had all the negative comments he was making said to him when he was a recruit and he would be saying exactly the same things again to the next batch of recruits after us or in army language NIGS (New Intake Grouped Soldiers).

The Troop Sergeant moved onto the next boy, the boy who had made the perfect bed block and slept on the floor all night to preserve it.

The troop Sergeant started to poke the bed block about with his pace stick as if it was too disgusting to touch with bare hands. "I've never seen a bed block as disgraceful as this one!!! With that he picked it up and threw it straight out of the window! Then he screamed "YOU MIGHT HAVE BROKE YOUR MOTHERS HEART BUT YOU WON'T BREAK MINE!!!!"

After the Troop Sergeant had inspected the whole troop the next place to go was the regimental barbers. The regimental barber cut the whole troops hair in about thirty minutes that tells you what type of haircut we got. I think the barber was also the county sheep shearing champion.

We then went over to the Medical Centre and queued up for injections. To this day I don't know what we were injected with but I remember this was done on several occasions. Speaking of the Med Centre if anybody went there for treatment for an injury no matter what it was the army medic would always prescribe Ralgex Muscle Rub cream. It didn't matter if you had a broken ankle, a headache, fever or the flu you would always come out with a tube of Ralgex, it became a standing joke if anybody had to report sick they would say, "I'm just going over to the

Med Centre to get a tube of Ralgex because they knew what was going to happen before they got there. The army must have had a warehouse full of out of date Ralgex somewhere but then again knowing what I know today some Tory politician probably had shares in the company!

We went for our first PT (physical training) lesson. All of our training subjects, Weapon training, first aid, military studies etc. etc. were all spread out over substantial distances around the vast camp so we always had to march quite a way just to start the lesson. PT was no exception we had to march a fair bit to get to the gym, which was a huge aircraft hanger. When we got into the changing rooms the PTI (Physical training instructor) would call the roll call and then say "you've got thirty f-kin seconds to get changed" and he absolutely meant it, we had to get changed like when you are very late for work and you dive out of bed and get dressed as fast as you possibly can, it was always like that getting changed for PT. After we got changed and went into the hanger there was a huge pile of boxing gloves on the floor, a subtle hint what was coming. For our very first PT lesson the head of the PT Department was going to take the lesson just this once. The head of PT was a civvie, but not any old civvie this was ex Staff Sergeant Gary Fuller who had recently retired from the army. He had just come from Ten Regiment RCT in Bielefeld Germany. Ten Reg as it was known was also referred to as "The Fighting Ten" because it was an absolute legend in the British army for winning anything and everything to be won for boxing in the army. It won the army boxing championships six years in a row in the mid 1970's beating every Infantry regiment including the Parachute Regiment. The main man responsible for their success was Staff Sergeant Gary Fuller a first class boxing trainer that anything he didn't know about boxing wasn't worth knowing.

Mr Fuller told us that all PT instructors were to be called "Staff "with the exception of himself who was a civvie so we were allowed to call him by his nickname. "What's your nickname?" enquired one of the recruits. "Sir" replied Mr Fuller.

Mr Fuller came over to me and asked me whether I was left handed or right handed. After telling him I was left handed he said to me "You are a Southpaw." He then went on to instruct me to lead with my right hand instead of leading with my left like orthodox fighters. So there you have it I received my very first boxing lesson from the legend himself Mr Fuller. (The so called boxing lesson I had at school didn't count)

After we had been moving around the gym a lot, practicing various boxing techniques taught by Mr Fuller it was time to put it into practice.

Mr Fuller called me out to the front of the class and asked me who I wanted to box. I had to think on my feet, we had only been here a couple of days and we didn't really know each other, if I picked the smallest weakest or easiest looking recruit I would be seen to be a bully and a coward but then again if I picked the toughest looking one I would be making a rod for my own back. So I thought to myself I'm probably going to get battered anyway, in for a penny in for a pound so I said out loudly and confidently'" I'll box anyone!" Mr Fuller looked genuinely surprised and repeated to the class, "This man will box anybody, who wants to box him?" As I was confidently watching all the recruits I saw all of their eyes drop to the floor, this is what happens when soldiers on parade don't want to be picked they think if they look down they will vanish or become invisible. This was a life lesson for me I have never forgot; I had successfully psyched out a squadron of recruits by shear bluff. This was a technique I have used many times over the years to get out of sticky situations, I was to use it many years later in South America when some blokes were trying to kidnap me only that time I wasn't bluffing but more of that later.

So I'm standing there with Mr Fuller and everybody is inspecting the floor. They all must have thought as I was so confident and didn't care that I must have experience and know what I was doing but it was 100% bluff, moral of the story; when ignorance is mutual confidence is king!!"

"Come on! Someone must want to box him," said Mr Fuller. Eventually one volunteer did put their hand up; it was a guy that was in my room that I'd been chatting to when we had arrived and were making up our bed blocks. So we gloved up and had a bit of a tear up before Mr Fuller called time. That was the only PT lesson we had with Mr Fuller and the easiest PT lesson I ever had at Junior Leaders.

We had our next PT lesson with the regular PTI's. There was a long thick rope that went from the floor to the ceiling of the hanger. At the top of the rope was a whistle to make sure you climbed to the very top and didn't cheat by not going to the top and coming down early. The whistle was covered in dribble, sweat and spit from all the other recruits. The rope we had at school was nowhere near as high as this one and I couldn't climb the one at school so logic told me if I couldn't climb the one at school I certainly couldn't climb this one. All the PTI's were built like brick shit houses and it was all real none of that steroid bollocks that posers take today these blokes were the real deal. "Up you go!" the PTI says to me, "I can't staff it's too high" I replied. "Look" says the PTI one of two things is just about to happen you are either going to go up that rope and blow the fu-kin whistle or I am going to beat the f-ck out of you. I went shooting up the rope and blew the whistle. I surprised myself. The PT staff knew more about us than we knew ourselves; the PTI knew I could do it but I didn't. We then moved on to press ups, sit ups, squat thrusts, parallel bar dips, star jumps etc.etc. with the PTI's marking down on a log how many we could do. They explained to us they wanted to see us improve all the time. They weren't interested in you pumping out fifty press ups every time they tested you, they were interested in the man who could only do ten press ups but next time they tested him he could do twelve or fifteen. Reading this you might think an obvious cheat is to hold back a bit and give yourself a decent gap to improve by. I'm afraid that won't work with army PTI's. Army PTI's are like Knowledge examiners you cannot pull the wool over their eyes they know who is giving it their all and who is holding back, that's the thing with the army it doesn't matter how fit you are everybody is pushed to their limit the PTI's always want more so it's a painful journey whoever you are.

Our weapon training was with the SLR (Self Loading Rifle). After we were proficient at cleaning it and stripping it down. We had to do it blindfolded, we were taught to take off our headdress and put the spare components of the rifle inside our headdress so they didn't get lost while we were blindfolded. Stripping down our rifle was timed by a training Sergeant with a stopwatch with and without being blindfolded. If we were slow the training Sergeant would always say, "F-kin get a grip there's 30,000 Chinese coming towards us." This phrase seemed to be used a lot and I found it interesting that they thought the enemy was Chinese considering that the figure eleven targets on the ranges had a soldier printed on them nicknamed "Ivan the Russian" which made a bit more sense to me as the cold war was very much on, although "Ivan" looked more like a German to me. We also did a lot of training with the LMG (Light Machine Gun). On range days we would go to the ranges on white army coaches or Bedford RL trucks or Bedford MK trucks. You would spend the whole day on the ranges and lunch was always exactly the same on range days, big metal chests provided by the Army Catering Corpse containing "Range Stew" which you had to eat from your mess tins and if you were lucky you might also get some bread and even an apple on a good day. Army ranges were all pretty much the same throughout the army, you spent half your time shooting and the other half down in the butts moving the wooden targets up for the soldiers who's turn it was to shoot, and then taking them down again to patch up the holes with wallpaper glue taken from a pot with a brush and then pasting little squares of paper taken from a book not unlike a raffle ticket book. The signal for the range commander to the people in the butts was an army field telephone with a wire that went to the butts and then a telephone at the other end for the people in the butts. You had to turn a handle on the telephone to make it ring. I can't remember the exact instructions on the range but there was always a sign by the phone that said something like: One ring- targets up, two rings- ready, three rings –targets down and then one day I saw somebody had written in biro at the bottom of the sign four rings- Let's fuck off. That did make me laugh because no matter how much you love shooting, range days are always a drag waiting around to shoot, or patching up targets in the butts, or picking up all the empty cases at the end, eating shit food. Then at the end you would have to have a parade and make a declaration that you have no live rounds or empty cases in your possession.

Our next PT lesson we had to do a BFT (Basic Fitness Test). The BFT is a standard test throughout the whole of the British army regardless of which regiment or unit you are in. It should be an easy test for anybody that is fit. Every single soldier in the army has to pass a BFT on a regular basis. It is by no means the hardest test you do in the army on the contrary it is the basic test all others are built from or increased from.

A BFT is just three miles. On a BFT you have to run as a squad (group) in three ranks for one and a half miles without breaking away. The PTI has a stopwatch and you must reach the one and a half mile point as a squad in exactly fifteen minutes by a combination of marching and running. When you arrive at the one and a half mile point you must turn around and run back on exactly the same route you came from individually. You have ten minutes and thirty seconds to get back and a PTI is waiting at the other end with a stopwatch to give you your own personal time when you reach him. Anybody over ten minutes and thirty seconds has failed and must take it again. For a BFT you had to wear a T-shirt, green lightweight trousers called denims and boots and puttees. I remember The PTI saying we wear boots and puttees because you don't say to the enemy hang on a minute while I go and put my trainers on. I am told they wear trainers in the army now for running. For this first BFT we had one PTI right up front with the "greyhounds" leading by example and showing us how it's done and then we had another PTI at the back that told us he was keeping pace to pass at ten minutes thirty seconds so if we stayed in front of him we would pass, he then went on to say that he wasn't going to let anybody fall behind him otherwise they would get his size ten DMS boot up their arse, true to his word he made sure we all passed. I was at the back but still scraped through with a pass. The PTI's lead by example one day we did a BFT one of the PTI's did the BFT wearing full kit and a respirator. That was the thing with the army nobody ever asked you to do anything that they couldn't do themselves or hadn't done in the past at least as hard and in many cases even harder.

We had a troop group photograph taken and the Troop Commander put it on the troop notice board and as the recruits left that couldn't hack it the Troop Sergeant put a cross across their face with a red marker pen.

We were doing regular drill sessions with the SSM (Squadron Sergeant Major). Our SSM was an ogre he was the stereotype of a Sergeant Major right down to the waxed moustache. He would put you in the jail for the slightest reason. Once we were doing drill with the band and the band had a Shetland pony as the band mascot and because the pony was acting up on parade he marched it down to the guardroom shouting out "Left, Right, Left, Right etc. and then made the guard commander fill out a charge sheet and jail the pony! He did it on another occasion when a fly was buzzing around the Squadron Offices he somehow managed to catch it in a jar and then took it down the guardroom and jailed it. Another punishment you could get if your kit wasn't up to the very high standards was show parade. If you were given show parade you had to report to the guardroom at 7pm in full number two dress and be inspected by the orderly Sergeant and if you were picked up on anything at all you had to report back the following hour and every hour up to lights out at 11pm. One day the SSM gave show parade to a boy in our troop for having a twisted bootlace on parade, that's how strict they were with your turn out.

The last meal was at five pm and all evening was spent cleaning the block (Called a "Bull" night) and washing and cleaning our kit and bulling our boots ready for parade in the morning.

One evening the Troop Sergeant came into the block and shouting in his usual aggressive voice, "I've got some bad news and some good news, the bad news is we have a CO's (Commanding Officers) inspection tomorrow so we will spend all night cleaning the block, rooms, stairs and ablutions, the floor in every room needs to shine like glass, the toilets and showers need to be cleaned and scrubbed with all the pipe work polished, all the mirrors need to be cleaned even though we shouldn't need them because the sinks should be so shiny you will be able to see your face in them".

After the Troop Sergeant had finished his long painfully brutal list of the terrible things of the night to come one of the boys said in a timid voice "'what's the good news Sergeant?"

"THERE ISN'T ANY!!!!!!!!!!!!!!!" replied the Troop Sergeant.

We were paid once a week in cash on pay parade. On pay parade The Troop Commander would sit at a desk at the end of the block corridor with the Troop Sergeant and the Troop Corporal standing each side of him. We would queue up in front of the desk and when it was our turn to be paid march smartly up to the desk with arms at shoulder height halt driving our leg into the ground, salute and then stand to attention while the Troop Commander counted out ten large green one pound notes. When the Troop Commander had finished counting out the notes we would have to say, "Pay correct Sir!" salute again, about turn driving our leg into the ground and march off. The rest of our pay would be held back in "credits" that we could only spend on leave. As soon as we were paid and the Troop Commander was out of sight the Troop Sergeant was in all the rooms having a whip round for troop funds (your guess is as good as mine). We spent our meagre pay on boot polish, yellow dusters, shaving foam, soap, shampoo, tooth paste, Brasso and the rest went on chocolate and sweets. Unlike regular army soldiers who spent their money on booze, cigarettes, hookers, gambling, tattoos and then the rest of their money they wasted!

Every Saturday morning we had a drill session followed by sports and on Sundays we were forced to go to church. The church was more like a chapel than a church. We were allowed to wear civvies to church but we had to wear a shirt and tie. Sunday afternoon was the only free time we ever had unless we were on exercise. Most army basic training is around ten weeks on average but in Junior Leaders it was a full year. We would go on exercise to Salisbury Plain, learning about field craft and digging in. Digging fire trenches in the middle of the night, then having to fill them in at a moments notice and then go marching on through the night map reading, running and generally getting f—ked about.

The PT was getting harder and harder we had to carry telegraph poles and logs for miles without letting them touch the ground. Running along the aircraft runways with them on our shoulders and out of camp through woods and up hills. There was a particularly steep hill near camp nicknamed "Heartbreak Hill' The PTI's would often make us go up the hill carrying another person. Some PT lessons we would all be issued

114

with a giant medicine ball each and then go for a run not letting the medicine balls touch the ground. Or sometimes we would go over the assault course in teams with logs not letting the logs touch the ground and if they did the team had to go back to the beginning of the assault course. If any man were slacking the whole troop would be beasted (army slang for being shouted and screamed at on parade doing drill or tortured with extra work doing PT). It's an old army trick to get people working to get teams competing against each other and the last team always gets beasted so you don't want to be the last person or the last team which makes you put in maximum effort.

I remember a lad in our troop complaining to the Troop Commander that the PT was too hard, he said to the Troop Commander, "Sir instead of the PT being so hard why can't they start easy and build it up slowly?" and the Troop Commander replied, "That's exactly what we are doing!"

As the red crosses were going over people's faces on the troop photo the empty beds were taken out of the rooms.

We used to go to a farm to do survival studies, learning how to live off the land and trap animals. This was run by a civvie. This civvie was an SAS Original, which means he did his selection in wartime not long after the regiment was formed. At this point anybody that has served with Special Forces will have their "Walt Radar" on full alert. A "Walt" is somebody that pretends they have served in the armed forces particularly special forces when they haven't. They are called "Walts" after the fictional character Walter Mitty that liked to fantasize. This was a time before Walts. With the reputation the SAS has today it's very difficult to describe to younger people a time when nobody knew who they were. This was before the Iranian Embassy siege, before their cover was blown to the public. The cover would have been blown eventually anyway with the Internet as the Internet has ruined everything that's supposed to be secret but at this time we had never heard of them and we were in the army! I will call him Mr P.

Mr P. just like my grandad would not speak about the war but he would tell us about army training in context with what we were doing. He humbly used to say that the SAS weren't so fussy who they took when he joined. He also advised us not to join the SAS as it was unpleasant and we should make a career of the normal army (The games dead?). As we were all only sixteen or by now seventeen years old and had never heard of the SAS anyway and MR P was as old as our grandads all of this went over our heads. It was only in later years I realised what a legend Mr P was and what a privilege it was to be trained by one of the originals. Here's the funny thing about time, Mr P was talking about his training days as if they were yesterday but as we were only seventeen and he was as old as our grandads he might as well have been talking about the ice age to us, but right now today I am talking about my training days as if they were yesterday and probably more time has passed from then until now than between Mr P's training time and when he was speaking to us. I think Einstein called this the elasticity of time. On our passing out parade Mr P was also on parade being presented with some award or other by the Brigadier. On the Parade the Brigadier mentioned publicly Mr P being in the SAS during the war, I don't think Mr P would be employed by the MOD and the Brigadier saying publicly what he did if Mr P was a Walt and especially at a time when nobody had heard of the SAS anyway.

We also studied NBC (Nuclear Biological Chemical Warfare) One day we were all sitting in a classroom studying NBC theory and I noticed the two training sergeants at the front of the class giving the lesson were both crying, their eyes were red and there was water pouring from their eyes. I was sitting at the back of the classroom. Baring in mind that recruits wouldn't dare even move in their seats without permission from the training staff I noticed everybody was jumping up out of their seats and running to the exit door of the classroom fighting to get out. Then it hit me, my very first experience of CS gas, My eyes starting streaming I could hardly breath, my lungs were filling up and I was fighting for breath, an extremely unpleasant experience and of course I followed everybody else out in double quick time. When the CS eventually went and everybody had settled back down, the training staff explained there were two reasons for what they did, the first one was to show us what CS was and to experience it so that we would recognize it if we came across it in Northern Ireland for example. The second thing they wanted to show us was it's harmless and you can hack it if you really have to so there is no need to panic if you experience it unexpectedly. I'm not so sure about the second bit I've experienced CS many times and I don't think I could ever do what those two sergeants did that day. Even after you've come out of the gas chambers and you get a whiff of it on your clothes it's terrible. So to train in NBC you put your NBC suit on known in army slang as a "Noddy suit" you then put on your respirator (Gas mask) complete with canister, put your hood up and boots and gloves. To check there are no gaps in the hood etc. you employ the "buddy, buddy system". Checking your mate while he checks you. You then all head over to the Gas chambers.

The Gas chambers are a small brick building. You all go in and the training staff burn CS tablets. You all walk around in a continues circle following each other, you then queue up in front of the training Sergeant take a deep breath lift your respirator and give your army number, rank and name exhaling all the time without taking a second breath and then run for the door. If you don't take a deep enough breath and have to inhale inside the gas chamber you are in the shit!

The reason you do this drill is because you need it for the other drills of changing your gas canister and eating and drinking drills. Basically if you need to change your gas canister you need to hold your breath while you are doing it, like wise to eat you need to take a deep breath, lift your respirator put some food in your mouth and then lower it again and then you can eat. You practice all of these drills inside the gas chambers. When you come out the gas clings to all of your clothes and it's best to go and stand in the wind.

We also learnt about decontamination taking self injected Naps injections and padding ourselves down with fullers earth.

Another easy PT lesson we had was the army swimming test. The army swimming test was easy. We were not the Navy Seals they just wanted to know we could swim. We all had to get in the swimming pool and tread water for two minutes while the PTI timed us. We then had to swim four lengths without stopping and that was it. Just like the BFT and the weapons test (shooting) you had to pass it or keep taking it until you did pass it otherwise it would be a red cross across your face on the troop photo.

We were now no longer NIGS (New Intake Grouped Soldiers) but were now PIGS (Previous Intake Grouped Soldiers), which meant there were new recruits around camp that came in after us.

A good day for me one day that highlighted how far I had come on from being the worlds weakest person was I was in the gym doing dips on the parallel bars with a PTI standing next to me with his arm vertical making a fist, you had to come down in line with his fist otherwise he didn't count. I can't remember how many I did but I think maybe around twenty five. After I had got off the bars there was a group of NIGS nearby with their PTI instructor. The PTI instructor called me over in front of his group of recruits and said to his class, "See this man here, when he got here he could hardly do one or two dips and now he is smashing them out, he is my hero, we are not interested in Superman we want to see improvement like in this man". I glowed with pride, some very rare praise. I had noticed that PT was getting easier but I hadn't really noticed how I had improved until that day.

Around this time there was a TV show called *Super Stars* which was a competition between athletes. The Judo Olympic Champion Brian Jacks always used to win the parallel bar dips competition. At this time in my life I couldn't possibly dream that one day I would train with Brian Jacks on a very regular basis. After I left the army I studied martial arts for many years. My chosen martial art after I had left the army was Wing Chun. There was a small group of instructors that would put on the boxing gloves and try out all of our techniques for real to see what worked and what didn't. We found at the time that the system was very good and effective while standing however its main weakness was if you had to go to the ground. This was all before mixed martial arts so to address this we contacted Brian Jacks and asked if he would train us in grappling. At first Brian wasn't interested and tried to put us onto one of his black belts but eventually we managed to persuade him we were very serious martial artists. So every Wednesday morning four of us would meet Brian in his sister's café in Orpington for breakfast and we would then go over to Brian's gym. We told Brian we weren't interested in standing Judo as we could take care of things standing it was just the grappling. So we would sit on the mats back to back and then turn as quick as we could and start ground fighting. We were well taught by Brian I learnt a lot from him but he could always do exactly what he wanted with me he was the Master.

One Wednesday Brian told us he had a gig to do at a Judo Club up in Accrington Stanley the following Sunday and asked us to go with him. The other three were busy so I went. It was a great day. We left at silly o'clock on the Sunday morning and drove up in Brian's car, we stopped on the motorway for breakfast and then eventually arrived somewhere around lunchtime. We were both treated like royalty even though I was just the tea boy.

The moral of this story is you just don't know what is going to happen in life or where it will take you. I'm still totally shit at dips but I'm good at choking people out.

The army has some great traditions one of them is that at Christmas all the troops have a big slap up Christmas dinner in the cookhouse and the Officers and senior NCO's wait on them. Another great army tradition is called Gun Fire. On Christmas morning the Sergeant Major and Orderly Officer and Orderly Sergeant go around all the barrack rooms serving tea and rum to the troops. Both of these traditions were observed in Junior Leaders.

As well as the very hard routine in Junior Leaders just like the regular army we had to do guard duty on top of all of our other work, duty and commitments. Guard duty is usually a twelve hour shift. We had to turn up at the guardroom at 7pm for guard parade to be inspected by the Orderly Sergeant and the Orderly Officer. To make sure we put 100% effort into our turn out sometimes there would be a Stick man. A stick man is an extra number that is not needed, so the Orderly Officer and/or Orderly Sergeant decide who was the best turned out soldier on parade and they get stick man and are stood down and don't have to do the guard duty. In the guardroom there are several steel bunk beds with PVC covered mattresses because the guard sleep in their clothes. The stags are usually two hours on four hours off. Off stag you just sit in the guardroom on the beds trying to get your head down and then on stag you go out for two hours. In Junior Leaders we went on stag in three's. We were each issued with an army torch and a very heavy long pickaxe handle with a lump of steel on the end. We were free to walk all over the vast camp. We were told to beat any intruders with the pickaxe handles. Sometimes the Orderly Officer would wait at the armoury, which was a mile or so way from the guardroom with a stopwatch, and call the guard out to see how long it would take them to get there. Another job the guard were responsible for was fire picket. There was a really long hose wound around a two wheel wooden cart painted bright red, we would have to run with it to any one of the many fire hydrants around camp of the Orderly Officer or the Orderly Sergeants choosing and attach the hose to the fire hydrant and again run with the hose to the specified position all under the eye of the Orderly Officer and all being timed by the Orderly Sergeant.

As we were now PIGS (Previous Intake Group Soldiers) instead of NIGS (New Intake Group Soldiers) we were deemed fit enough for the Brecon Beacons in Wales. The Brecon Beacons exercise was run from the Adventure Training Wing. We got out of the army four tonne Bedford trucks at the bottom of the Brecon Beacons one January morning. Despite it being January it was a lovely bright sunny day. We set off immediately up a very steep footpath at the side of a hill. We had warm windproof clothing, a Bergen, sleeping bags, three man tents and army rations and just one litre of water each on our belt kit. I remember looking up the steep incline and thinking to myself it doesn't seem far to get to the top, it shouldn't take us long. When we got to the "top" we found ourselves at the "bottom" again and looked up to see a similar view as we had seen an hour earlier. And so it went on climbing the steep mountain. After a while I started to notice it was getting colder, and then it started getting misty, then it became foggy. We walked for miles and miles. The training staff knew the Brecon Beacons like the back of their hand because they did this every single week with all the different troops of our regiment. They explained that from time to time we might see the odd solitary man go shooting past us with a small house on his back carrying a rifle without a sling. We were told these were SAS selection soldiers, the idea of having no sling on your rifle was so you couldn't just throw it over your shoulder and march on, it forced you to carry it properly at all times. I thought to myself that's the second time I've heard about this lot. On we marched. We only stopped once at midday for our lunch that consisted of army compo rations. We set off again, mile after mile, the training staff pointed to a dead sheep in the stream and said, "That's why we don't drink from the stream up here". On we marched. We eventually stopped at the edge of a rock face. This was to be my very first abseil in the army. The very experienced training staff got every one of us to abseil down to the bottom. I always find that the worst part of abseiling is that first lean backwards and then after that it's a great feeling. After abseiling to the bottom off we set again. We marched over all terrain, one minute we were on gravely tracks and the next minute we were walking across these giant mounds of tufted grass. We were starting to get really tired now. The training staff were shouting out words of encouragement. "Put your mind in neutral and your arse in gear!"

It was dark now; we had been marching over the Brecon Beacons all day now from early morning. I was sweating like mad carrying the weight from my Bergen and I had drunk the last of my water hours ago. I was now seriously thirsty, later in the army with experience I learnt to ration my water but right now I was in the shit (or chin strapped in army slang). We crossed over a narrow stream and there was a waterfall splashing over a rock. It was exactly drinking height, I saw it as a gift from God and it was just too tempting. I noticed the rest of my troop were ignoring it, I don't know why, maybe fear of being beasted by the training staff, or maybe they had rationed their water more wisely, I took the decision to drink despite the Training staff warning to the contrary, I didn't take the decision lightly I was well aware of the risk, I had drunk from a stream as a much younger boy and it made me very ill, there was also a lady on our council estate with a hunched back who got Polio as a child from drinking from a stream but I was so desperate it felt like I was going to die if I didn't. That night was the thirstiest I have ever been in my life before or since, I can't describe how lovely that water tasted and luckily the Training Staff didn't see me in the dark. The water seemed to give me a new lease of life and an hour or two later we reached the summit and set up our tents in the pitch black. The mess tins and hexi blocks came out and after our rations we fastened the tents for a good nights sleep we were exhausted. If I tell you I slept at the top of the Brecon Beacons in January you would probably think, I bet that must have been bitter cold but the God's honest truth is I don't remember being cold at all and that night was the best nights kip I've ever had, I slept like a log. The next morning the training staff gave us a generous lay in if I remember rightly. Extremely rare for Junior Leaders Regiment, in fact I think it was the only time it happened. After eating the last of the rations for breakfast we set off back to the trucks. Luckily we didn't follow the same route back, we went a much shorter route straight down the hills and mountains and found ourselves with the trucks and tea urns.

Our accommodation in camp was reasonable as was the food but often we would go on exercise to training areas where the accommodation was literally left over from National Service. One weekend we were at one of these places and they had the old steel grey lockers as well as the steel beds. One of the boys in our troop was a very heavy sleeper so for a laugh one morning before breakfast we carried his bed with him sound asleep still in it and put it in the middle of the parade square and also his steel locker next to it. He was still asleep when the Sergeant Major came on the parade square for early morning parade. He got us all on parade for a beasting, "WHO ARE THE F-KIN CLOWNS DISRESPECTING MY PARADE SQUARE?" "WELL?" "WHO F-KIN WAS IT?"

We were all guilty so we weren't going to grass any individuals and nobody was going to own up either and take the whole blame.

There was a football pitch in the far distance. "LIFT YOUR F-CKIN WEAPONS UP ABOVE YOUR F-KIN HEADS WITH YOUR ARMS STRETCHED OUT STRAIGHT AND RUN AROUND THAT F-KIN FOOTBALL PITCH IN THE DISTANCE, LAST MAN BACK HERE I WANT TEN GOOD PRESS UPS AND IF I SEE YOU LOWER YOUR ARMS I WILL F-CKIN SNAP THEM OFF AND BEAT YOU OVER THE HEAD WITH THE SOGGY END.........GOOOOOOOOOOOO!!!!!!!!!!!!!!!!"

When we had all run around the football pitch in the distance and got back to the SSM as the last man was doing his press ups the SSM growled, "WELL WHO WAS THE F-CKIN SMART ARSE THEN?...............NO?...........OFF YOU GO AGAIN LAST MAN BACK I WANT TEN GOOD PRESS UPS!!!!"

"PUT MORE F-KIN EFFORT INTO IT!!!!!!! IF YOU DON'T KEEP THOSE F-

CKIN ARMS STRAIGHT I'M GOING TO F-KIN RAM THIS F-KIN PACE STICK THROUGH BOTH EARS AND RIDE YOU AROUND THE SQUARE LIKE A F-KIN MOTORBIKE!!!!!!!!!!"

This went on for most of the morning. Moral of the story was you can't beat the army system and you'll never get the better of the SSM

Another place we went to on adventure training was Cheddar Gorge. This was the place we went pot holing. Cheddar Gorge was full of caves. We went pot holing all through the caves. One minute we were crawling through very tight claustrophobic tunnels with a real risk of getting stuck and the next we were in big open caves. We also came across rocks inside the caves that we had to abseil down that was the part I really enjoyed.

We also went to Snowdonia doing pretty much the same as we did at the Brecon Beacons. We did a fair bit of rock climbing in Snowdonia with ropes. I remember being taught that you should never use your knees in the crevices and gaps because if you use your knee you are stuck, you can't move up but if you make the extra effort and put your foot there instead of your knee you have leverage to raise your leg, they were very strict on this rule and it makes sense if you think about it but when I watch rock climbers on the TV using their knees instead of their feet I want to shout at the TV. Once we were going over a mountain with no ropes and it had ice on it, I slipped on the ice and nearly went over the edge, a quick thinking Staff Sergeant grabbed my wrist just in time. I think the army's attitude to health and safety was; there is no health and safety in war and that's what we are training for.

Also on Adventure Training we did capsize drills in a canoe. I don't remember actually going anywhere in canoes only doing the capsize drills. The funny thing is I did canoe capsize drills a few times in the army but never paddling in a canoe. It was like the army only wanted to give you the shit part and not the good part.

Our last part of training in Junior Leaders Regiment at Colerne before moving onto our trade training was driver training. We all had to pass our driving test. The driver training was for one week only starting on Monday morning with the driving test on the Friday. We were put in groups of three to a car taking it in turns to drive. All the cars were civvie cars with civvie driving instructors, however all the test examiners were army sergeants! I think the army wanted to make sure we passed!

On our passing out parade we were all suited and booted in our best Number two dress uniform. It was a proper special day with all of our family invited. On the parade we had bayonets fixed and had to stand to attention for long periods of time. A handful of soldiers fainted, we had one boy faint in our troop and unfortunately the bayonet went through his chin. It's not as bad as it sounds and fortunately he was OK.

All cabbies when describing the Knowledge say they wouldn't want to do it again but they are glad they did it and that is exactly how I would describe Junior Leaders Regiment.

We had finally passed out, losing many along the way. We had been beasted seven days a week for a year; the anecdotes I have written were just the tip of the iceberg. We had done an awful lot considering we were just seventeen years old.

The Army School of Mechanical Transport

In the army you are always a soldier first and a tradesman second.

After passing out at Colerne we were now fully trained infantry soldiers it was time to go on a very well earned leave and then with freshly issued travel warrants report to Driffield in East Yorkshire for our trade training and being in the RCT that meant driving, and lots of it. At Driffield we were still Junior Leaders (detached)

The ASMT (Army School of Mechanical Transport) was another former RAF airfield at Leconfield a few miles from our Junior Leaders Accommodation in Driffield. Our first morning on the parade square with the SSM;" Listen in gents. Welcome to Driffield you have now finished your army basic training but we still expect you to be smart on parade, we don't care what you put on your boots, we don't care if you use Klear, seal or any other f-kin floor cleaner you like, you can even f-kin paint them for all I f-kin care but they will be shining like a dollar up a sweeps arse!!!!'

So now we had learnt our first army secret, not all regular army soldiers bulled their boots, they used a piece of cotton wool dipped in a floor cleaning liquid with *klear* being a particular favourite quickly wiped over the toe and the heal of your working boots and hey presto! Instantly bulled boots. Thinking back to Colerne I remember seeing some stuff flaking off of the Troop Corporals "Bulled" boots, at the time I thought it must be polish flaking off but I now know it was probably Klear. Klear and Seal were used widely in the regular army in the 1970's/80's but never in training with the exception of some training staff, both of these popular products of the time are unavailable today.

At Colerne it was strictly no alcohol but now we were detached there was a troop bar on our camp we were allowed to use. Even though the beer was definitely watered down we were still underage, we were now all seventeen but at this time the army was a law unto itself. There wasn't much health and safety with the exception of the ranges, the army was shit hot when it came to range safety, sometimes we even put up a red flag somewhere.

The SSM went on to say, "You will be doing long hours of driving so you will need your full ration of sleep, that means lights out at 11p.m sharp and then sleep all the way around until.......(and then I thought F-ck me he's going to give us a lay in every morning)........6a.m!!

After breakfast we would collect a packed lunch supplied by the Army Catering Corpse and get one of the white army coaches to ASMT at Leconfield. ASMT was huge with virtually every cap badge in the army there. There has always been a lot of rivalry between the different army regiments. The army has always loved acronyms so of course army humour has always given them a different meaning than was intended by the army. I will list a few so you have an idea of what different regiments called each other:

We were the RCT   Royal Corpse of Transport (Rickshaws, Cabs and Taxis)

Before we were the RCT our Regiment was called RASC   Royal Army Service Corpse (Run Away Someone's Coming)

REME   Royal electrical and Mechanical Engineers (Royal Engineers Minus Education)

RAOC   Royal Army Ordnance Corpse (Recruit Any Old C-t)

ACC   Army Catering Corpse (Army Concrete Company)

And so it went on………

At leconfield we had another parade with Leconfield's SSM. Straight after parade we went to the vast lorry park to pick up our vehicle's Bedford TK four tonne trucks and meet our HGV (Heavy Goods Vehicle) instructors. In civvie street you had to be twenty one to drive an HGV vehicle but the army at this time being a law unto itself you could hold an HGV licence at just seventeen years of age. Surprisingly all the HGV instructors were civvies except one who was an RCT WO2 (Warrant Officer 2nd class/Sergeant Major). And trust my luck I was the only soldier to get a f-kin Sergeant Major as my instructor, although to be fair he wasn't too bad except the day I ran over all the cones on the airfield on the reverse parking exercises, he called me everything except a Christian!

Some mornings we would spend an hour or so on the camp airfield runways doing tight manoeuvres around cones but most of the time we would leave camp and spend the whole day driving around Yorkshire. We would drive through Hull City centre, miles and miles around the Yorkshire countryside, through towns and villages, up and down steep hills practicing hill starts and at the end of the day we would go back to Leconfield park up and get the army white bus back to Driffield. And we would do this same routine for several weeks until the instructor thought we were ready for our test. After we had passed our HGV test we would swap our Bedford TK truck to a Bedford MK truck and start the Combat Driver Training.

On Combat Driving there was a cross country obstacle course of steep muddy hills and muddy pools of water and rough terrain. Several years earlier while I was at school I had seen John Noakes on the TV programme *Blue Peter* driving an army truck on this exact same course and at that time I had never even thought I would go anywhere near the army let alone join it.

We went around the course as a convoy and I remember just as we were about to start the training instructor saying, "If only your mum's could see you now eh?"

Joking aside he was right, here we were just seventeen years old looking the part in our smart combat uniform, neatly shaped berets in massive army lorries driving across very rough terrain. It was a time to be proud and enjoy the army.

Over the coming weeks we learnt everything about combat driving, driving at night, driving across all terrains, driving in convoy, maintenance, loading and sheeting loads and cargo etc.etc. Then came learning how to cam up our vehicles (camouflage them so they couldn't be seen from the air). First we went in convoy to the forest. We all found a parking space between trees and then we were taught how to cam up. The first thing to do was get rid of any shine, you did this by pulling in the trucks cab side mirrors and covering the windscreen with black hessian sacking and trapping the hessian in the cab doors. You then covered up all the lights, headlamps indicators etc. with more black hessian. After this you got on the roof of the canopy and cab and unfolded a cam net across the roof and draped it down all sides with a generous overlay on the ground. The cam net was like a green squared fishing net with artificial leaves fastened all over it. You now had a giant oblong box with a cam net draped over it so the next stage is to break the shape up otherwise from the air it would look like a perfectly squared oblong bush with flat sides and top. You break the shape up by putting long wooden poles underneath the cam net and with the cam net hooked onto the top of the poles you push the poles out away from the vehicle so no part of the cam net is touching the vehicle and the net is sagging from pole to pole at all different heights and distances so it is a very irregular shape just like trees and bushes. When done properly the truck is "garaged" under a cam net that has a very uneven shape that from the air would look just like a bush and the shape of the truck would be completely hidden.

Just to make sure we got plenty of practice, as soon as we had put the finishing touches to cam up our vehicles the training staff would shout, "CRASH OUT"!!!!!!!!!!!! This meant we had to de cam and pack everything up as fast as we could go and move location. As soon as we got to the new location a very short distance away we would start all over again. This went on all night, it reminded me of back at Salisbury Plain where we had to dig shell scrapes and fire trenches all through the night. Finally the training staff called Endex (End of Exercise) and we headed back to camp. After finishing with trucks we had to drive all different army vehicles, Land Rovers, Staff Cars etc. I remember we had to do stall start drills in a Land Rover on an almost vertical hill on the combat driving obstacle course. We would drive up the hill with an instructor and then he would tell us to stop the vehicle near the top without using the clutch so the Land Rover deliberately stalled and then with the vehicle still in gear we would move it forward on the key.

After finally finishing our trade training we were known as TSA (Trained Soldier Available). We now had to wait to see where we were going to get our first postings as fully trained regular soldiers. One of my mates got Ten Reg. We were winding him up because Ten Reg was the most brutal Regiment in the Corpse, it was the boxing regiment and it sent all the best boxers there as well as any bully, hard case or psycho that couldn't be tamed anywhere else. And then another three got Ten Reg and I was one of them. After we were given our postings we got issued with more army travel warrants and went on leave. After leave those of us going out to Germany had to report to RAF Hendon where we caught a flight To RAF Gutersloh. I was looking forward to the flight, as I had never flown before.

Chapter Three

Ten Regiment RCT

(The Fighting Ten)

My friends and I landed at RAF Gutersloh airport one very hot summers afternoon. The usual army coaches were waiting to transfer us to our various postings. After being driven on the "wrong" side of the road for a while my three friends and myself got out at Bielefeld and struggled through the big white gates of Ten Regiment RCT with all our kit. We reported straight to the guardroom. The guardroom's first point of access was a kiosk with a sliding glass window, on the back wall were many black and white photos of various past and present Ten Reg boxers with their hands being held up in the air by referees standing over various knocked out soldiers from all regiments, Ten Reg never lost at boxing. We were told that the regiment was currently in Northern Ireland so we would be joining the rear party. Ten Regiment had an important role in Northern Ireland and did regular tours there. Their role was to supply armoured transport and drive the Infantry foot patrols. The vehicles were armoured Humber pigs. As a Ten Reg driver you could find yourself attached to any Infantry Regiment. Ten Reg were always in the middle of some of the worst of the troubles. Sometimes they even went under cover, a mate said one day he was driving his Pig and a mate of ours pulled up at the junction next to him in a civvie mini wearing civvies with a Browning pistol stuck inside his jeans, he was working under cover (Sneaky Beaky in army slang).

My three friends and I were kept together and were given a four man room in the squadron blocks. Our Troop Sergeant was a tough Irishman from Northern Ireland. He was very straight talking and was very funny even though he didn't mean to be. He would shout out on parade, "You f-kers go to Northern Ireland for a few f-kin months and come back with a f-kin medal, I've lived there for thirty f-kin years and got f-ck all"!!!!!!!!!!

Another time I was on guard duty and when I answered the guardroom phone I said the usual, "Good morning sir Ten Regiment Guardroom" and as soon as the Troop Sergeant heard my voice he said, "Ah Cabman, get off the f-kin phone and put Corporal J on!" You had to laugh at his directness.

Life on the rear party was pretty shit, the days were spent on the vehicle park checking over the ten tonne trucks. Our Squadron Square was a massive parade square fenced off by lines of ten tonne trucks. Every day we had to sweep the leaves off the vehicle park / parade square and then check all the oil, water tyre pressures on the trucks everyday even though they hadn't been anywhere since they were last checked the previous day.

We were warned by the sweats (Soldiers With Experience And Training) that had been at Ten Reg for a few years to watch ourselves from bullies when the regiment got back from Northern Ireland. They told us stories of how the regiment was obsessed with fighting. On a Saturday night the thugs would leave their false teeth in a glass of water by their bed spaces and go down town looking for trouble. They caused absolute havoc down town picking on any regiment they could find. Soldiers from other regiments would keep out of their way so when Ten Regiment couldn't find another Regiment to fight they would turn on each other fighting inter Squadron!

There was a big RMP (Royal Military Police) unit in Bielefeld just up the road from Ten Reg and Ten Reg would keep them permanently busy. I could never work out why the army didn't chuck out these very troublesome soldiers but I later learnt that the army valued them highly because although they were a complete pain in the arse in peacetime when there was trouble they were right up for it, then they became more valuable than some peace time soldiers that were very good at a lot of military skills like marching and drill and shooting etc. but not necessarily as good when there was trouble.

I remember The Regiment coming back from Northern Ireland. I was on the gate on guard duty and let the big white army coaches come through the gates. They were all in combat uniform with their SLR's (Self Loading Rifles) and they all looked a lot older than me although in reality it would only have been a few years.

That night the whole regiment went down town. My three friends from Junior Leaders and myself had an early night because we had been on guard duty. We were awoken that night by one of the returning soldiers from Northern Ireland kicking our room door down. Each room had a table with four steel legs screwed to the bottom of it. The drunk ripped one of the legs off and proceeded to beat the four of us with it. He got the biggest one of the four of us and gave him a black eye. Not long after a big Scottish Corporal came in our room and seeing the state of us wanted to know who did it, he explained that if you were new at Ten Reg it was customary to take a "slap" however he didn't agree with it and said it was his duty to break the "tradition". So he asked us again, "Who did this"?...... silence.....".Are you f-kin deaf? If you don't tell me I will be taking my anger out on you!" So we told him........With that Corporal B kicked down the bully's door and gave the bully a "Glasgow Kiss!" Now the Bully had a black eye and his lips were like balloons.

The next morning the four of us were in the SSM's office. The SSM said to us, "The blokes a f-kin nobody why didn't the four of you chin him?". So we got a bollocking from the SSM for getting beaten up. I overheard an officer asking the Troop Sergeant what's happening to the bully? The troop Sergeant said' "It's all in order Sir Corporal B has dealt with it".

134

And that was the end of the matter. Just another day at Ten Reg. I saw some photos of Corporal B on the squadron notice board with some children in Northern Ireland doing some hearts and minds stuff I got the impression he was a good bloke.

The Northern Ireland tour wasn't a good one because one of the lads didn't come back. I remember being on parade when everybody got their medals (everybody got the active service medal for a Northern Ireland tour) and the man's dad collected it. They named one of the accommodation blocks after him.

Another duty we had to do at Ten Reg was guard the cookhouse all night because some of the lads would come back from town pissed, break into the cookhouse and start cooking all of the food! I had to do this duty not long after arriving at Ten Reg. There was an army camp bed on the floor and all you had to do was keep the doors locked and sleep. Ten Reg's cookhouse was infested with mice and cockroaches. When the lights were off you could hear all the mice squeaking and when you turned the lights on you could see all the cockroaches scuttling away, so sleeping on the camp bed on the floor wasn't a good idea so I put it on the tables to sleep on. It wasn't long into my duty until one of the regiment's Welsh boxers unoriginally called "Taff" was tapping on the cookhouse door for me to let him in. Taff was one of the 1970's boxing team that won everything for boxing six years running, he had just been busted from Corporal back down to Driver for beating up a couple of Military Policeman so the best move was to let him in. Taff was pissed and went straight over to the hot plate got a load of ingredients and started cooking as if he was in the Army Catering Corpse, you could tell he had done this many times before and left as quickly as he came. Nothing was ever said so a bloody waste of time that duty was!

I got put on the RP staff (Regimental Police). I did twenty four hour shifts on duty with forty eight off. We did two hour stags on the gate and four hours off in the guard room. The Jail in the guardroom always had prisoners being Ten Reg. We had a Corporal Guard Commander and the Provost Sergeant was the boss with of course the RSM being the overall boss. The Provost Sergeant was Sergeant Jimmy McMann and Ten Regiments boxing trainer an extremely tough character. He was well known for beasting the prisoners by letting them hit him three times and then he would hit them once and knock them out!

It went something like this to a new prisoner "So you think your some sort of f-kin hard man do you?"

Prisoner   "No Sergeant"

Jimmy Mac   "Why are you in my f-kin jail then?"

Prisoner   "Don't know Sergeant"

Jimmy Mac   "I'll tell you what I'll do if you think you're so f-kin hard, I'll give you three hits and then I'll hit you just the once, I can't be fairer than that"!

Jimmie Mac "HIT ME"!!!

Prisoner "I'm not going to hit you Sergeant"

Jimmie Mac   "You might as well because I'm going to hit you anyway but I'm a fair man so I will give you a chance"!!!!!!!!

And then the prisoner knowing he's going to get slapped anyway would have a go and Jimmy Mac would be keeping count, smiling and saying "you've now had number one" and so on. He would only hit them once and they would be out cold. He wasn't a bully he never did it to anybody that he didn't think deserved it or needed it. I know he wasn't a bully because he gave me the biggest bollocking of my life and never laid a finger on me. He actually gave me three bollockings for the same incident.

Ten Reg had a back gate as well as a front gate. Unlike the front gate the back gate had a sentry box with glass panels and a door; it was a bit bigger than a phone box because you could just get a chair inside. It was winter and it was cold and nobody said don't use the sentry box, what would you have done?

So I've not long started the stag and I'm sitting in the sentry box and in comes Jimmy Mac in his civvie car. He slams the brakes on and gets out. I've never seen a man in such a rage, eyes bulging, red face, veins bulging out of his neck, screaming one inch from my face, "WHAT THE FUCK DO YOU THINK YOU'RE DOING?!!!!!!!!" Then he proceeded to shout and scream at me for the next five minutes. I can't remember what he was saying because in the army once you've established where you f-ked up (In my case sitting in the sentry box) you just take the bollocking on the chin and it goes in one ear and out of the other.

So after I had finished my two hour stag and went back to the guard room I expected Jimmy Mac to have forgotten it or at least calmed down, I couldn't have been more wrong, he started to bollock me again but this time just in a normal army parade ground loud shout not the psychotic screaming and shouting like before "WHY WAS YOU F-CKIN SITTING INSIDE, YOU SHOULD'VE BEEN ON THE F-KIN GATE....." etc. etc.

It didn't end there, several hours later at the end of my shift he gave me a third bollocking this time in the form of an advisory, fatherly, calm chat, "You know what you did wrong don't you?

Me   "Yes Sergeant"

Jimmy Mac "Have you been to Northern Ireland yet?"

Me   "No Sergeant"

Jimmy Mac   "Well it's f-kin serious, people get f-kin killed when you f-k up"

Me   "I've learnt my lesson Sergeant it won't ever happen again"

Jimmy Mac   "Good lad, off you go then."

Being on duty for twenty four hours with forty eight hours off there was obviously three teams on operation. That year our team fell on Christmas day AND New Years Eve! Was this fair? No of course not but that's army life nobody said it was going to be easy. On Christmas morning there was two of us on the gate and it was snowing and the RSM (Regimental Sergeant Major) must have been going around giving gun fire to the troops because he came over to us on the gate with a flask and gave us the traditional rum and tea. The RSM was in number two dress and was wearing brown gloves because he had some fingers missing. The word was he had them blown off in Northern Ireland but it's not a good idea to question the RSM to confirm it.

While I was in the guardroom some of our mates would tell us about previous tours of Northern Ireland, one of my mates was telling me about another one of our mates who was a light weight Ten Reg boxer, he was well known for winding people up and when he was in Northern Ireland he was attached to the Royal Marines. He used to always be saying to them you lot can't make up your mind if you want to be in the army or the navy, it was all banter and I'm sure the Marines gave back as good as they got. Another day he said to them why are you the only people that wear the same colour beret as the WRACS (Women's Royal Army Corpse) I'm sure that one must have gone down well!

Another mate told me he was attached to the Paras (Parachute Regiment) and they went out on patrol one night and parked up. The Paras said it's all going to kick off soon but don't worry we will deal with it all we want you to do is stay with the vehicle and when it all kicks off just pop the street lights out with your SLR. My mate said he wasn't bothered about being fired at because he had been fired at before but he was absolutely shitting himself in case he missed the bulbs in the street lights when he was supposed to blow them out. I was cracking up when he was telling me.

I was recently on one of those closed veteran groups on social media and one of the veterans on there said that his regiment wanted to improve their boxing team so they went to Ten Reg to do some sparring and Ten Reg had to get their heavyweight boxer out of the jail to spar. I didn't comment but I had to smile to myself. Ten Reg memories.

The following year I was posted to a large Royal Signal Regiment on detachment from Ten Reg.

Chapter Four

The Royal Signals

In January 1982 I was posted to a large Royal Signals Regiment that had six squadrons plus HQ Squadron. Soldiers from Ten Reg RCT were posted to MT Troop (Mechanical Transport) HQ Squadron. We had a vehicle park of Bedford MK trucks a couple of Bedford RL trucks, lots of Land Rovers both long wheelbase and short wheelbase and a load of trailers of all sizes for both trucks and Land Rovers. Next to the vehicle park we had our servicing bays and our troop was responsible for servicing all the regiment's vehicles as well as supplying transport around the regiment. Each of the six squadrons also had their own squadron garages and vehicles. We had another vehicle park the other side of our troops offices. On this park we had the POL (Petrol, Oil, Lubricants) Pods . Pods were tanker trucks that refuelled all the Jerry Cans that were used for refuelling the Regiments vehicles on exercise. We were out in the field on exercise nine months of the year! Sometimes we went on exercise for a week, came back to camp for a week and then went back out on exercise for another week, sometimes we would be out for three or four weeks and sometimes the siren would go off in camp in the middle of the night and we would crash out on exercise for weeks at a time so we were on permanent standby meaning our personal kit as well as our vehicles had to be ready at all times. The work was interesting and varied as we swopped jobs all of the time. I drove officers around on opps. I drove trucks carrying everything from personnel to rations and ammunition. Sometimes I worked in the servicing bay servicing all the Regiments vehicles and I also worked in the tyre bay changing tyres on trucks and Land Rovers.

A few months before I arrived at the Regiment the IRA cut through the camp's fence at its weakest point down in the woods and blew up one of the accommodation blocks. The accommodation block they blew up was the Sergeants Mess. As we were all on exercise there was just one Staff Sergeant sleeping in the block. The way our rooms were laid out were a window with a radiator directly below it and then a bed next to the radiator. In the explosion the radiator fell on top of the Staff Sergeant acting as a shield saving his life and then all the bricks and rubble fell on top of the radiator. So nobody was hurt but a reminder to take security seriously, I could now see for myself why Jimmy Mc Mann gave me such a bollocking back at Ten Reg. A year or two after this incident I was walking back to MT Troop's accommodation block after lunch and noticed in our corridor that was always kept immaculate and clear that there was a very suspicious bag left there all on it's own so I immediately went up to the guardroom and reported it. The guardroom didn't f-k about and immediately cordoned the area off and called the Royal Engineers Bomb Disposal in. We all stood around while the Royal Engineers sent in a remote control robot with tank tracks and a gun on it that I was told fired water. They blew the bag up and it turned out it was a German Civvie maintenance workers tool bag. The RSM (Regimental Sergeant Major) was on the scene and shouted out "Who reported this?" after I had told him it was me he said' "Well done! Stay alert gents, stay switched on!"

When we went on exercises they were huge. There would be whole "villages" of us in the woods. You would have huge tents as cookhouses; you would have the Sergeant's Mess, the Officer's Mess etc.etc. Generators for power, hundreds of vehicles and the whole lot would be completely camouflaged from the air. There was also a complete blackout at night so when you went in the Opp's room as you opened the door of the wagon the lights would automatically go out, then you would walk through a black curtain and then all the lights would come back on as the door was shut and there would be all these high ranking officers around maps and on radios. As soon as your vehicles came into the woods there was a switch you turned on the vehicles dashboard that stopped all of the vehicles lights, indicators and brake lights working so black out was maintained. One of the best jobs I had was Recce (Reconnaissance). My boss was a large well built man from London who was also the Troop Staff Sergeant he was a brilliant character and a practical joker and wind up merchant; in fact I'm still friends with him today. One day we were sitting in the opp's room with the 2i/c (Second in command of the regiment). The film *The Long Good Friday* starring Bob Hoskins as a London gangster had just come out and we had all seen it including the 2i/c. In walks a private soldier that needs to give a message to the 2i/c but he forgets to salute so the 2i/c immediately turns to Staff H and says, mimicking the character and scene in the film, "I think a bit of respect is called for Razors!" So Staff H bollocks the Private, "Don't you salute the 2i/c of the regiment Private!!!" of which the Private soldier immediately springs to attention and salutes the 2i/c. It probably doesn't sound funny here but the timing and everything at the time was perfect. Razors was the gangsters "heavy" in the film and in the film there's a scene with a trolley jack where Bob Hoskins says "I think a bit of respect's called for Razors" and then Razors kicks the jack away and nearly crushes the poor geezer with a jacked up car that's no longer jacked up. The nickname stuck and after that a few of the officers called Staff H "Razors" so for the purpose of this book I will refer to him as Razors.

Razors used to love winding up the regiment's CO (Commanding Officer). On exercise in the rations we used to get a small packet of two or three NAFFI biscuits, they were either Bourbons, custard creams or digestives and you didn't know which ones you would get it was pot luck. Then one day on exercise the RSM happened to mention to Razors that the CO preferred the Bourbon biscuits, in fact he was very partial to them. So one evening in the CP (Command Post) Razors put out a signal to all units, "All units, all units, listen in, we have been advised by the NAFFI that all Bourbon biscuits issued on this exercise are very out of date and are also seriously contaminated, all personnel who have had the misfortune to be issued with these biscuits are to return them with immediate effect to the CP, this order does not affect any of the other biscuits". In the army you do as you are told immediately and without question so pretty soon there was then a massive queue of soldiers handing in their Bourbon biscuits to Razors. Razors put all the biscuits in a Hay Box. An army Hay Box is a big steel box with a lid that looks a bit like an ammo box that the Army Catering Corpse use to store hot food in e.g. "Range stew". When the CO came over to the CP with the RSM later that night Razors said to the CO, "Would you like a brew Sir? a cup of tea Sir?"

CO   "That would be nice Staff"

Razors   at the same time as opening the lid on the Hay Box, "Fancy a Bourbon Biscuit Sir?"

The CO looks down at the treasure chest mountain of Bourbon biscuits in stunned silence and then walks off shaking his head chuckling to himself, chewing on a Bourbon biscuit of course.

On Recce we used to go up to the American Airbases quite a bit looking for hard ground locations to make a change from forests. The first thing Razors would ask is where's the stores? Then his second question was "Who's in charge?" (Of the stores). He would then proceed to do all kinds of wheeling and dealing with Buckshee (spare) kit. We would be sitting around on exercise looking as cool as f-k with American mess tins, American sleeping bags and even American watches. I was even driving the Catering Officer around once on exercise and I overheard him as you do (You London Black cabbies know exactly what I'm talking about now don't you?) boasting to a couple of other officers " Yes Razors is going to get me one of those new American porta loos for my civvie caravan." I was smiling to myself because there would be a good chance I was going to be there when he "acquired" it.

As I have already said Razors liked to wind the CO up. One Saturday night when there was one of those suited and booted Officer's Mess do's when the wives have to wear a ball gown and everything is formal and full of pomp Razors got hold of the CO's staff car driver which was easy to do because our troop was responsible for the CO's staff car so Razors was the drivers boss. Razors stood the driver down and told him he was going to take care of it. So at the appointed hour instead of the CO's driver turning up at the CO's house to take the CO and his wife to the Officer's Mess a big American car turned up with an American soldier in full American ceremonial uniform with the white gloves and everything saluting the CO in the American way. The CO came out laughing and then shaking his head and said straight away Razors has got something to do with this. Of course Razors had arranged it with one of the American airbases.

We dreaded autumn because our vehicle park was surrounded by trees and every autumn the leaves from the trees would fall every day, which meant we were permanently sweeping them up. As soon as we had swept them all up and the square was looking immaculate more would be falling. One army saying is "Join the Navy and see the world, Join the army and sweep the f-ker" The whole troop would be going across the square in an extended line with bass brooms. This was even pissing Razors off and he didn't have to sweep them. So one day he rang the Army Air Corpse that were in Detmold if I remember rightly. He asked the Army Air Corpse if any of their helicopters were flying over our camp at any time. They confirmed they would be flying over next Tuesday afternoon. So Razors arranged for the helicopters to fly above our vehicle park and then lower themselves over the trees as low as they could get. The helicopters blew all of the trees leaves off leaving them totally bare. We were able to clean all the leaves up in one go, job done. I've got a lot of respect for helicopter pilots, it's not as easy as it looks I took one helicopter flying lesson just once years later at Shobdon airfield in the UK flying a civvie Robinson helicopter. I found it quite difficult especially hovering; it felt like being in a chair as a kid on the big wheel when one of your loony mates is rocking it like f-k. I was glad to get back down I don't mind being a passenger but flying ones not for me I was shitting myself.

Our Regiment along with lots of others went on a big exercise in a huge training area called Vogelsang. Vogelsang was where they trained the Nazis in the war and you could still see huge carved eagles in the brickwork with big empty circles where the swastikas had been taken out. Our troop did our usual stuff at Vogelsang supplying all kinds of transport along with our drivers. There were a lot of TA reservists on this exercise. The TA were always very keen because unlike us who lived and breathed it 24/7 permanently this was their annual main gig so they understandably wanted to make the most of it. Rightly or wrongly most of us regular soldiers dismissed them a bit like London cabbies do mini cab drivers. So one day on this exercise I am driving a Sergeant Major from one of the Infantry Regiments, I can't remember which one exactly because there were loads on this particular exercise but I think it was the Cheshire Regiment. So I'm driving him all around the training area in a Land Rover with him next to me. On account of there being so many TA on this exercise I get it in my head that he is TA. Then all of a sudden a huge eagle comes swooping past us and the Sergeant Major is all excited saying, "F-k me!!! Did you see that!!!?" and he's ducking his head trying to get a better look as I casually look over at him trying hard not to be impressed and said "Yeah we get a lot of them out here" as if it happens fifty times a day. The Sergeant Major immediately new what my game was and sussed me out immediately and said, "How long have you been in the army son?"

Me   "Three years"   (Note the lack of "Sir" which would never
happen addressing a WO2 Sergeant Major in the regular army)

Sergeant Major   "Not bad, I've just completed twenty years in the
army!

Me   awkward silence, then, "Oh, Sorry Sir I thought you were TA"

Sergeant Major   "TA?   No they are a right bunch of f-kin
muppets!!"

Moral of the story, don't ever underestimate anybody not even the
actual TA, I'm sure there must be some really good TA soldiers out there
but as I said at the beginning we weren't politically correct whatsoever
in the army of those times.

One day on this same exercise we had to deliver a truckload of grenades
to the grenade range for one of the Infantry regiments to throw. For
some reason they never showed up so Razors said, "Fuck taking this lot
back we will throw them all down the range ourselves and go back
empty" So we threw the whole f-kin lot down the range. Razors kept all
of the grenade pins. When a soldier throws his first grenade he usually
keeps the pin as a souvenir and to look cool, hard and warry some clip it
to the zip of their combat jacket, not all soldiers of course just some. So
Razors links all of these pins together and makes a chain as long as a

skipping rope. When we got back to camp he wraps the grenade pin chain around his neck several times like *MR T of the A Team* and hides it under his combat jacket. He then walks around camp looking for NIGS with a grenade pin on the zip of his combat jacket and then every time he sees one he stops them and says, "Thrown a grenade have you son?" pointing to the single pin on their combat jacket "Yes Staff" "Well I've thrown a few myself!" He would then undo his combat jacket unravel the huge chain of grenade pins and start skipping with it, you should see the looks on their faces a mixture of shock, amusement and embarrassment.

There was also a lot of Belgium army on this exercise needless to say we went back to camp with a few Belgium army sleeping bags and other assorted bits of their kit.

Being on exercise so much I became an expert at camouflaging my vehicles. None of the cam net touched my vehicle so I was able to drive out of the forest leaving the cam net exactly where it was and come back at night and drive straight back into it like a garage. In my time in the army I worked with many European armies. I can tell you none of them were anywhere near our league. The way they would cam their vehicles was to just throw a cam net over it, loads of shine and glare on the windscreen and the vehicle just looked like a box or a vehicle with a net draped over it, It was pathetically bad. When I was in the army no British soldier wanted to be connected or anything to do with any EU army we knew what they were like from experience.

When we had a bull night in the block cleaning all the rooms and toilets for a Troop Commanders inspection, if a young officer was posted in an old army trick was to melt a bit of chocolate and smear a bit on the wall near the toilet and then when the Rupert (officer) came to inspect he would see the smear on the wall and look at the troop Corporal and Say "What's this Corporal?" The Troop Corporal (In on the joke) would then lift a piece off with his finger lick it and say, "It's shit sir!" The Rupert would then turn to the Troop Sergeant (also in on the joke) and say, "Sergeant?" The troop Sergeant would then also lift a piece off with his finger, lick it and say "It's definitely shit sir!!!"

In April 1982 The Falklands War started. We had never heard of the Falklands and didn't have a clue where it was. They told us it was cold and that if we got issued with warm clothing that's where we were going. A mate of mine tells me a load of us went into the troop office and all volunteered for the Falklands and the Troop Sergeant was going ape shit because we were saying it's shit here we would rather be in the Falklands, although I must say I don't remember and I hate the cold so I don't think I could have been with them. The Falklands was all over in a few weeks anyway so none of us went in the end apart from a few of the lads from the other squadrons in our regiment.

We used to guard places that were top secret, so secret that we didn't know what they were and what we were guarding. One place we guarded was a square about the size of a football pitch with two high security fences all the way around the square, One inside the other one so any would be attacker had to scale two fences, a tower on each corner, flood lights and a grass bunker in the middle. We were told the sight was American not British and the rumour was it was American missiles. I had five magazines of twenty rounds one hundred in total that's quite a bit of firepower just for guarding a glorified football pitch. What was interesting was the difference in our rules of engagement (legal rules of when we can shoot people) to the Americans. We were issued with a green card with the rules of engagement clearly printed on them. It said if anybody tries to touch the fence give them one verbal warning to stop in the English language (Bearing in mind we were in

Germany this was no nonsense stuff). If they ignore the warning shoot to kill.

We were told the American rules of engagement were to fire three warning shots in the air and then if this was ignored a single shot to a limb (Not shoot to kill).

For me this was the massive difference between our armies. I was proud to belong to an army that didn't f-k about if a job had to be done we did what needed to be done without f-kin around.

We had a soldier in our troop who went down town one night and came back with crabs. The next morning on parade when the Troop Sergeant gave the order to "Fall out" instead of marching forward the whole troop marched along sideways like crabs. We gave M his own toilet at the end of the line of toilets in our accommodation block with his name painted on the door and a sign saying, "Please don't throw match sticks down the toilet just in case the f-ckers can pole vault out!"

What I loved about the British army above everything else was it's unique sense of humour. As the work could be very dangerous we got by on black humour. Our CO had a great sense of humour because he had been in the SAS for five years. The more dangerous the job the blacker the humour. If somebody shouted out, "Aaaah I've lost my leg!!!" you could be sure somebody would answer, "No you haven't it's over there!"

We kept very fit. Our Troop Commander was a Captain that had come through all of the army ranks from Private soldier. He was an ex RSM so was very strict, he also used to play Rugby for the army. He took us for a run every Tuesday and Thursday morning before morning parade. I was now one of the fittest in our troop, only one other soldier in our troop used to beat me when we had a BFT.

Every Wednesday afternoon the CO had the "CO's Fun Run" whereby the whole regiment that were not on essential duty went on a run all over the hills.

I was now in the Squadron boxing team. My boxing was nothing special; advertisers were keen to put advertising on the soles of my boots!

As the CO was from the SAS we had dealings with them that we might not have otherwise had. Signals are a big deal in SF (Special Forces). Units usually work in very small groups of experts depending on what the job was, maybe a Medic, a linguist, a demolitions expert and almost always a signalman. We had guys floating around camp from 22 SAS Regiment with the now famous sand coloured beret and fire/dagger cloth cap badge. I assumed they were on signal courses it wasn't the etiquette to ask. We had a guy from 22 SAS attached to us who I will call Dave. Dave was of normal size and build and the only difference in appearance to anybody else around camp was his beret and his moustache and hair was longer than anybody else's. I read somewhere that the SAS only wear their beret inside secure military premises. I can tell you in the early 1980's this wasn't the case, at least as far as Dave and his mates were concerned, they were always wearing their beret around camp, on exercise and even down town on NAFFI break or dinner break to nip into the bank. All soldiers of the British army are very highly trained but SF are obviously trained to a much higher standard. Here's a true story that highlighted that fact for me.

One weekday at 3am the Regiment were awoken by the Siren to crash out on an unexpected exercise. We were always on permanent standby so when this happens the regiment comes alive. Everybody is up getting dressed as fast as they can, the first up are running up and down the corridors banging on everybody's doors. The team of "Active Edge" duty drivers are already dressed in combat uniform and are driving around the army married quarters getting everybody up. The armoury is opening. The cookhouse is opening, trucks are being started, loaded and there are soldiers from all the squadrons tying cam nets and poles to the roofs of all vehicles. You can hear Sergeant Majors and NCO's from all the different Squadrons shouting orders. Soldiers that live out are continually arriving in their civvie cars. The place is a very loud, buzzing, organised chaos.

Our Armoury was a brick built, bombproof building with a very heavy steel door located on the edge of the main parade square. Everybody has an armoury card to present to the armourer in exchange for their own personal weapon. Everybody's weapon is personal to them because it has been zeroed (adjusted) to them down the firing ranges. As an RCT driver your personal weapon is usually an SLR (Self Loading Rifle). Being attached to the Royal Signals my personal weapon was changed from an SLR to a SMG (Sub Machine Gun). I was delighted not because the SMG is a better weapon on the contrary I preferred the SLR as an effective weapon but because it was more compact I could throw it over my shoulder (Your weapon never leaves you, it is a serious chargeable offence if you are ever caught with your weapon out of arms reach). The SMG still got caught up in cam nets while you were trying to cam your vehicle but it was much more manageable.

I walked across the now busy parade square over to the armoury that was almost opposite my accommodation block and joined the queue to draw my weapon. I found myself directly behind Dave. I was curious to know what weapon he would draw, I didn't have a choice but I knew in the SAS you could choose your weapon to suit the job. I imagined Dave would probably draw some super duper space gun that I had never seen before. When Dave got to the armourer I was surprised and pleased to see that he had drawn a bog standard SMG exactly the same as mine.

We were issued with a thick brown cord like sling. The sling had a brass clip at each end to fasten to the two steel eyelets each end of the weapon. In the middle of the sling was a brass buckle to adjust the sling that wasn't needed, in fact the brass buckle was usually stuck and ingrained into the sling where it had never been moved.

I watched every single man in front of me draw their weapon, immediately put the sling on, throw the weapon over their shoulder and stroll down to the cookhouse where the Army Catering Corps were flat out cooking the traditional full Monty British army breakfast to feed the whole regiment before we deployed. There were no exceptions; every man did exactly the same until it got to Dave.

Dave drew his weapon exactly the same as everybody else, Dave attached the sling exactly the same as everybody else, and this is what separated Dave from everybody else, instead of slinging the weapon over his shoulder, he walked down the corridor of the armoury with the weapon in the firing position, moving and sliding the brass buckle up and down the sling to get the most effective, natural and comfortable firing position. He made something so simple, and yet so important look really professional.

Something we had a laugh about on exercise with Dave. I was driving a Commanding Officer from one of the Armoured Divisions around the exercise location in a Land Rover. He was boasting to some other officers that were sitting in the back how much of an ogre his RSM was and how he was going to beast everybody on exercise. A couple of days later the RSM in question noticed that Dave needed a haircut (the SAS always had longer hair at this time in the army) instead of giving Dave a bollocking and telling him to get his haircut like an RSM would usually do he told a Sergeant to go and tell Dave that the RSM said he should get a haircut. Dave thought it was hilarious. Dave's rank was Trooper (private) he said to the Sergeant, "You can tell the RSM that I don't bite and if he wants me to get a haircut he can come and tell me himself!" We all had a laugh at the RSM's expense.

Our CO arranged for 22 SAS to do a recruitment talk and slideshow. You cannot join 22 SAS from civvie street but you can apply to do selection from any regular army unit. A couple of good mates of mine wanted to go so asked me if I wanted to go with them. I wasn't bothered about going but it was an escape from our usual stuff so I went along just for something to do.

We were in a small room with around roughly thirty of us. There was a Captain from 22 SAS he was a very large well built man with a hard reddish face, I recognized him from on exercise. He was accompanied by a Sergeant of normal size and build also from 22 SAS. Our CO was sitting at the front and although he was wearing the cap badge of the Royal Signals he had the SAS parachute wings on his uniform. Our CO was the first to take the floor and he started to talk about the town of Hereford. Saying it was famous for cattle and had it's own football team etc.etc. And then eventually said," it's also famous for the SAS of which I spent a very short time, five years", and everybody gave a little chuckle. He then handed it over to the SF Captain who gave our CO a proper salute; I could tell from the body language that the two SF guys really respected our boss.

The film *Who Dares Wins* starring Lewis Collins had not long been out and the very first slide was a still from the film of actors in black kit abseiling from a helicopter. "If you're here because of this gentlemen it's not the best reason to be here". Apparently since the film came out they had had a spike in people doing selection.

"The very first thing you do as you get off the train at Hereford is a normal BFT. Yes a normal BFT. Not a BFT blindfolded with both legs tied together (Everybody laughs). Believe it or not we do get people fail it, although we haven't had anybody fail one for a while now they're starting to get the message".

They show another still from the glamorous cinema film and explain the job's not glamorous at all, in fact it can be very shit and boring as we do a lot of recce and surveillance, they then went on to tell us about one of their guys dug in for days or even weeks near a bridge and he had to count how many people went over the bridge on foot and how many vehicles went over. After every five or six slides there would be a soft porn model posing with large boobs "Just to make sure you're all still awake" said the DS (SAS Directing Staff responsible for selection and training). The humour on this talk was brilliant; they showed a slide of a skinhead hooligan with a tattoo on his head making an aggressive rude gesture, "We're not interested in the rebel" then a slide of guardsmen in full number two dress marching on parade, "We're not interested in the poser". I looked at our boss and he was cracking up.

" I want to clear up a myth, there is a myth that we take a quota, a quota of 2 or a quota of eight or a quota of ten, I can tell you gentlemen there is no quota, we will take as many good men as we can get our hands on, if everybody can pass selection we take everybody, if nobody passes selection we take nobody it really is as simple as that, the reality is between 90 and 95% fail."

They went on to explain the course, how the weights and distances would increase everyday. More jokes and soft porn slides followed.

"This course is all about not giving up, if you give up at any time you are immediately off the course and you will never ever be invited back, there is no second chance, however if you are injured and we think you have potential we will invite you back to have another go".

People die on selection, if you find yourself on the Brecon Beacons in a snowstorm and a colleague dies the advice is to use them as a windbreak until the storm goes and then use them as a sledge to get to the bottom.

So did I do SAS selection? No I remember what happened the last time I attended a recruitment slide show with a Captain and a Sergeant!

Chapter Five

South America

This book was originally only going to be a book on the Knowledge of London but after I had finished it seemed a bit on the thin side so I thought I would put a few army memories in to beef it up a bit and now that seems to have lead on to a few South American anecdotes. After coming out of the army I did a lot of martial arts and various bits and pieces. One of my hobbies is languages with the strongest one being Spanish by far. So I was lucky to be able to travel South America off the beaten track.

Costa Rica

Central America

My travels actually started in Central America. I flew out to San Jose Costa Rica. In the bed and breakfast I was staying in San Jose the landlady was very proud of the fact that she had a hot water shower. "The shower has hot water" she boasted. When I went for a shower I noticed it was a coldwater shower with a thin live electric wire running along the top of the showerhead heating the water to lukewarm as it came out.

The next day I headed for the jungle. It took me a day by boat to get to a mini leisure resort of a few cabins in the middle of the jungle.

The cabins were of a good standard with showers and were right on the edge of the river. There was also a small swimming pool by the ranch type bar. There was a sign by the swimming pool and also at the wooden jetty at the edge of the river that said "Beware of Crocodiles". I imagined giant crocodiles walking past the swimming pool as I went for my morning swim. The truth is crocodiles don't grow that big in Costa Rica, at least I never saw one. In fact I never saw any and was starting to think the signs were some sort of bullshit joke and then I watched the chef come out of the cookhouse with a bag of cooked chicken, he walked along the wooden jetty where we had arrived a day earlier and promptly threw the chicken by the jetty in the shallow end of the river bank, he then banged a wooden broom hard on the side of the jetty multiple times and then a f-kin great crocodile came for the chicken. I say big crocodile it was actually only about seven or eight foot but it is a true story. During the day the place looked like a piece of paradise, there were toucans in the trees along with spider monkeys, and lizards running up the paths. Then when the sun went down I thought I would sit by the small bar next to the jetty and have a few drinks. The mosquitoes were proper man eaters I got bitten to death despite having insect repellent. I noticed they didn't bother the natives at all. Then when I went back to my room there was a huge insect that looked a bit like a giant grasshopper crossed with a cockroach on my bedside cabinet staring at me with an aggressive expression and moving antennas and then there was something similar in the shower and then before long the place was like a zoo. It was so bad I didn't dare get between the sheets. I tried to get some sleep lying on the bed fully clothed but the place was worse than the cookhouse at Ten Regiment.

There were a couple of racoon type animals fighting right outside my door and a load of jungle noises in the distance as well as right up close.

The next day I went deep into the rain forest. The rain forest was very muddy and wherever you looked it looked exactly the same in any and all directions. The guide showed us a very large tree with really big roots and told us that's where the natives go when there is a hurricane. I also saw several of the little red poisonous dart frogs that Costa Rica is famous for. Our guide told us they are extremely poisonous and you only have to touch their skin to die. He went on to say that when the Spanish *Conquistadores* came the native Indians only had to wipe their arrows on the frogs back to be sufficient to kill the invading Spanish. What surprised me about these frogs were how small they were, they were only about the size of your thumbnail.

All told Costa Rica was pretty uneventful apart from all the wildlife. I went to this butterfly zoo that was basically an open part of the rainforest but with a giant green fine mesh covering the butterfly farm/zoo area. It was really colourful there seemed to be every butterfly in the world there all under one net. I also went to the beach where they had a turtle conservation programme going on but unfortunately it wasn't the right time of year.

Ecuador

Ecuador is right on the equator hence the name Ecuador. Being on the equator it gets light at around 6a.m and dark around 6p.m every day and this is indefinite it is the same all year around and doesn't change with the seasons. The apartment I was staying at in Quito couldn't have been more central. My apartment was directly opposite Parque La Carolina. I could actually see the old 1940's airplane that is in the centre of Parque La Carolina.

In town like much of Latin America there was a large Catholic presence with a large winged statue of the Virgin Mary. The locals joke that she is the only virgin in Quito. There were also over fifty churches in a very small area so you could go to a different church every day of the year if you wanted.

I really liked Quito despite it being dangerous in a few places. The laws were pretty straight forward and common sense. For example the highway code (London black cabbies will love this one) It was explained to me that in Quito a red traffic light means stop for traffic and go for pedestrians and a green traffic light means go for traffic and stop for pedestrians, and that's it. This traffic law is taken very seriously so if you f-k up for example you are a pedestrian crossing the road on a green light you will be run over and there will be no legal comebacks, and this was explained to me by a lawyer friend not some geezer on a bar stool. So the liberty taking cyclists in London that ignore red lights and do as they please would simply be mown down in Quito. One downside was that there was no vehicle insurance so drivers involved in road traffic accidents would have to try and work it out between themselves. In the back streets of Latin America a popular and common thing to do to protect your property was to smash loads of glass bottles and then cement the jagged edges and slithers of glass sharp side up along the tops of all of your walls surrounding your property, it was very cheap, effective and green from a recycling point of view. When I explained to my friends that they wouldn't be able to do that in the UK they couldn't understand why not so to emphasise my point I told them that if someone breaks into your house in the UK and you seriously hurt them you can be prosecuted, they couldn't and wouldn't believe me, they explained to me that if that happened in Ecuador if it was a clear cut case of breaking and entering burglary and the home owner dealt with the burglars it would be an open and shut case with no court case needed!

My first day down town I nipped into McDonalds in the middle of the afternoon and the place was exactly as you would expect it, busy with people with their families just like any other McDonalds anywhere in the world, the only difference in Quito was two private security guards that looked like police in black kit armed with semi automatic weapons. Again I was told if anybody tried to rob the place they would be shot and due to the amount of witnesses there would be no need for a court case.

One weekend I decided to take a trip to the Papallacta hot springs. Basically you take a bus up the mountains and the springs are natural hot volcanic pools, you pay a small fee and then get changed just like the swimming baths and relax in hot rocky pools in the mountains.

After swopping buses a couple of times from Quito I found myself at the public transport terminal at the bottom of the mountains. The bus had a crack right across the windscreen with bits of faded Sellotape on parts of it, bald tyres and the driver stunk of booze. The driver being pissed didn't bother me too much because in Latin America despite it being supposedly illegal all the men drink and drive, in fact their attitude is if you don't drink and drive you're a wimp who can't hold your drink! It was more the bald tyres going around a tight mountain on a slippery dirt track with a fall over the mountain where you would end up very dead that concerned me more! Then I told myself get a grip this is Latin America and this is all normal and part of the experience. As we went up the mountain I couldn't help thinking about the bus that went over the mountain with the gold in the film *The Italian Job* because the mountain was very similar. As we were going up and up and spiralling around the mountain we passed another bus on it's side with what appeared to be dead people and some very sombre people waiting for some sort of rescue. As we passed we nearly went over the side ourselves. I was very glad to get to the summit. The hot springs were absolutely fantastic; they were like natural swimming pools with sharp jagged rocks around the sides. What I found interesting was that there was just one sign in the English language saying beware of the sharp rocks. In Ecuador I quite rightly didn't see any signs anywhere in English but here was a single sign in English that wasn't repeated in Spanish. It made me think. They obviously think it's not worth putting a sign in Spanish because if anybody from the Spanish speaking world hurts themselves they are not looking to blame anybody but themselves for not taking more care. Conversely in the English speaking world if anybody gets hurt they are automatically looking for somebody to blame by default.

One evening I decided to go right over the other side of town for a drink (I don't drink alcohol I prefer to have my wits about me especially in South America). I went into a small but busy bar in the back streets of Quito. I ordered a drink and all drinks in this bar were one American Dollar. I went to hand the barman five dollars and he said, "Sorry we don't have any change you need the right money". Luckily I had plenty of one Dollar notes on me so I passed him one, sat on a stool at the bar and didn't think anything else of it. As I watched people buying drinks, they were all paying with one Dollar notes and anybody that offered anything larger was told exactly the same as me. I sat at the bar thinking and then I thought to myself if everybody is paying with one Dollar notes how come there's no change to give back? Curiosity got the better of me and I just had to ask the barman. He explained to me that as we were in such a dodgy area we were at very high risk of being robbed so no money at all could be kept on the premises, so all money was passed out the back to be transported elsewhere at regular intervals. The "as we are in such a dodgy area" part was news to me. When I eventually started to make my way back to my apartment in central Quito I took a wrong turn and instantly "felt" I was on a very dangerous street. Despite it being the early hours of the morning the street was busy with rough looking druggy type people. My gut feeling was telling me to get out of the area as fast as I could. There was a small group of men standing around a fire contained in a steel bin on legs. They called over to me, "hey do you want a taxi?" pointing to a beaten up car that wouldn't even have made it as an illegal taxi, all the hairs stood up on the back of my neck I knew what was coming, posing as a taxi driver is one of the favourite methods of kidnap in South America. At this particular time neighbouring Colombia was the kidnap capital of the world. Kidnapers liked to hang around tourist spots after the last buses and taxis had gone posing as the last taxi or bus. I even had a friend that was nearly kidnapped in Colombia by the kidnapers posing as police. I told them I didn't need a taxi and carried on walking, one of them started to walk towards me, I was at the prime of my martial arts having trained everyday for years and was quickly weighing up the situation, as I was taking my opponents measure I noticed he was armed with a wooden club, it wasn't a proper baseball bat but a makeshift lump of wood around the same size as a baseball bat, I also noticed it had nails sticking out of it, probably more likely it was an old fence post or something rather than a deliberate attempt to make a weapon. I turned to face him I noticed that the others weren't following him and they were a distance away. I lowered my head to protect my jaw and looked through my eyebrows as I had done many times before both inside and outside of the gym, I positioned myself for a pre emptive strike, I didn't say anything but I gave him a look that said if he took just a single step forward it was going to end badly for HIM. It's a look you cannot recreate in the gym you have to be in a life threatening situation. I was in a similar situation to all those years ago when I was made to box as a sixteen year old standing in front of an army squadron only this time I wasn't bluffing and I had already committed. The guy looked me in the eye, turned around and walked back to his friends. In martial arts it's what they call the art of fighting without fighting. I walked off at a fast pace. A real taxi driver slowed down and shouted to me to get off the street as I was in a very dangerous area, he got me back to my appartment safely. There are many reasons why I chose to do the Knowledge one reason was that taxi drivers had got me out of the shit a few times in dodgy situations and I wanted to give something back, being a London cabbie there is opportunity to help people that need it and with my life's experiences I can tell who needs it and I love to help out when I can.

Peru

In South America there is a huge presence of the indigenous native people. They can be seen everywhere in their very brightly coloured blankets with the women with long plaited black hair and strange top hats. I always assumed they spoke Spanish like everybody else in Peru even if they did have their own dialect. I was at a market in Lima Peru trying to negotiate a price on a leather belt when I discovered the indigenous man selling it couldn't speak one word of Spanish. I discovered their language is called Quechua. A few examples of English that comes from Quechua are, Condor, puma, llama, coca.

I was waiting for a flight from Lima to Cuzco. I was told the flight was delayed because there was a lot of fog around the mountains and a new strict law had only come in that week that there would be no flights unless the mountains were completely clear of fog. Before they would fly if they were "reasonably" clear but the week before a plane hit a mountain killing the pilot and all of the German passengers. I was happy to wait and grateful it was this week and not the week before.

I used taxis a lot in Latin America and the golden rule was to first make sure the taxi was licensed and then when you were satisfied it was safe to get into negotiate a price before getting in. There is always an exception to every rule and the exception to this rule was Cuzco Peru. In Cuzco the taxi service was first class for passengers, I'm not sure if it was so good for the drivers. There was a fixed price of two Soles to go anywhere in Cuzco. Everybody knew this so you could just jump in a taxi without mentioning any prices because you both knew what the price was going to be. So if you asked the price before the journey you were telling the driver that you were a tourist and didn't know the two Soles rule. I am glad to say out of the hundreds of taxi journeys I took in Cuzco only one driver asked me for three Soles. Two Soles in 2003 was about 20p. The lesson in honesty I gave to the driver was to legal him by giving him the three Soles he asked for but accompanied with the spiel of, "Here's three Soles, two Soles for the ride and one Sol as a tip, I normally give 10 soles to drivers that ask me for two Soles but since you have asked me for three soles I will give you three soles". I hope he learnt from it. Using taxis a lot in foreign countries I know what passengers want and expect so I try to give them what they hope for and expect in London.

Cuzco was a nice place you would often see the colourful indigenous people walking through the narrow streets with a llama or an alpaca on a lead.

It was in Cuzco that I discovered that the Coca leaf is not drugs or cocaine. Up in the Andes sometimes the oxygen is a bit thin and you can get a bit short of breath. The locals recommended I take raw coca leaves either directly chewed in the mouth or a handful of raw leaves put in a cup with boiling water added and drunk as a tea that they called Ma-te (pronounced ma as in mat and te as in ten). I was a bit reluctant at first but the locals reading my mind explained that the raw coca leaves has nothing to do with drugs and very little to do with cocaine, they said to make cocaine you would need a room full of the leaves plus a load of chemicals and stuff to add and then it would need processing. The raw Coca leaves had a long list of medicinal benefits from curing altitude sickness, tiredness, fatigue, upset stomach the list went on and on. The leaves were sold almost everywhere, at the markets the indigenous people would be standing next to open sacks of it selling it by the bag. I noticed nearly all the indigenous people chewed it raw like tobacco but I preferred to take it as ma-te. Every bar and café sold ma-te, when ordered the waitress would put a handful of leaves taken from an open sack, put them into an empty mug and pour boiling water over the leaves in front of you. Being in South America I learnt a lot about propaganda from the UK and USA.

I went across the Andes with some American and Canadian guys I had met up with. A lot of the terrain reminded me of the Brecon Beacons, I remember thinking to myself I could have done with some Coca leaves back in my Brecon Beacon days.

My American/Canadian friends said they were going to the Inca ruins of Machu Picchu at the weekend and invited me to tag along if I wanted. We caught a medium sized mini bus from Cuzco for the long journey. The mini bus was almost full and we were lucky to get a seat. After about a forty minutes drive we stopped at our first bus stop. I assumed this would be to let a few people off the bus but nobody got off and more people got on! An indigenous man with a homemade cage of live chickens took the last remaining seat next to me! We stopped at a bus stop every half hour or so for more people to get on. I learnt in Latin America they have no concept whatsoever of too many people or "full" as far as vehicles were concerned. If they managed to get a family *and* a fridge on a moped imagine what they thought was acceptable for a mini bus! Every bus stop yet more people were getting on, by now the side doors were left open and people were hanging out of them, I started to think that this was a serious attempt to break all records of getting the most people on a mini bus, then I discovered we would have lost! An identical mini bus as ours overtook us with as many people as us but there were around six people on the roof! We eventually got to a town that I can't remember the name of but we had to get the night train to Aguas Calientes, which is at the foot of Machu Picchu.It was now dark and as we waited at the fairly primitive train station there were some indigenous women selling what resembled "Range Stew" from a large cauldron. The price was about three soles (60p at the time) and was served on standard china plates with a ladle with a steel spoon supplied. I noticed that after the customers had finished eating, the dirty plates and spoons went into a plastic bucket of cold water and as a new customer ordered, the plates and spoons were produced from the said bucket. My colleagues took "advantage" of the local offering but I had eaten with the Indians before in the Andes and I was out of action for a couple of days so decided to give it a miss this time and stuck with the rations I had brought with me.

When the train eventually arrived it was surprisingly modern and fast for the time. We arrived at Aguas Calientes late at night and as we pulled into the station there was an army of touts all standing on the rail tracks (There were no station platforms) and all claiming to represent the best and cheapest hotel in Aguas Calientes. We followed one of the touts to our hotel. Our tout was right about the cheap part. It worked out around two pounds a night in English money, which was very cheap even by Latin American standards. The room was presentable but I didn't trust sleeping between the sheets. I had a shower needless to say it was freezing cold but you can't really complain when you're paying two quid a night. The next morning we were up bright and early and walked up to Machu Picchu. It's one of those places where no amount of photographs or filming is going to do it justice you just have to go there.

Rather than walk back down we took the bus down. As we started to make our way down the steep mountain a young boy of around twelve years old came out of the bushes in front of the bus and started waving at us. I'm sure like myself nobody on the bus thought any more of it. Then a few minutes later as we turned the corner of the steep mountain's road the same boy jumped out and did the same again. This happened again and again around a dozen times as the bus got lower and lower down the steep mountain. By the time we got to the bottom he was soaking in sweat. Unless he had eleven identical brothers with just the right amount of sweat on each level, he had abseiled down each rock immediately after the bus had passed him each time with the abseil getting longer every time as the mountain got bigger and bigger towards its base. At the bottom he got on the bus with a hat hoping for tips. He was covered in sweat and really earned that money, I think everybody gave him a generous tip, he deserved it.

We got the train back to Cuzco in daylight. The panoramic views and scenery are the best I've seen on a train journey. When we got back to Cuzco the mountains are too steep for the train to come down so the train has to stop and then shunt backwards for a while before stopping again and then going forwards again. This shunting backwards and forwards has to be done a few times to get down the mountain.

Argentina

I flew from Madrid as I often did when going to South America. This time the destination was Buenos Aires. They say that Buenos Aires is the Europe of South America and I would agree with that. Buenos Aires didn't seem like the rest of South America and it was the place I blended in the most, as I didn't dress like a tourist and always walked like I knew where I was going sometimes people would pull up in a car and ask for directions. I couldn't help notice there were a lot of men around my age with limbs missing obviously from the Falklands war so I wasn't expecting to win any popularity prizes but I have to say I liked the people from Buenos Aires and I didn't get any problems at all from the people that knew I was English, it just confirms normal people are generally good it's just governments and politics that are usually the problem.

One of my favourite souvenirs of South America is a pair of photographs I have. The first one is of the Casa Rosada (The Argentinean Presidential Palace) I took showing all the high security, massive steel barriers and heavily armed guards and the second one is of myself sitting at the Presidents desk with the Argentinean flag behind me and a view out of the window of where I took the first photo. Now I could come out with all sorts of stories of how I came to be sitting at the Presidents desk but like the rest of this book I will tell the truth as it happened. There is no great story, what happened was I booked a tour to see inside the Casa

Rosada. The tour was vetted I had to leave my passport with them for a day or two and then when I got security clearance I was allowed to be shown around. The Presidents office is not part of the tour but as the President wasn't in the guide asked the small group of us if we would like to see his office, when we said yes we would the guide had to go off somewhere and get further special permission. After a little while the guide came back with the green light. So as we all went in the Presidents office I was first in and I happened to be standing by his desk. When we all left the room the guide was first out leaving me at what was now the back so I cheekily jumped in the Presidents chair and got someone to get a quick snap.

I had a friend at the time in London that was into Argentinean Tango. As I was walking the streets one day I noticed a couple of Tango Dancers on the pavement outside of what I presumed was a dance studio. I thought it would be nice for my friend if I filmed the two authentic Tango dancers on the streets of Buenos Aires for my friend back in London. So I approached the dancers and told them I would give them a tip if they could just do some nice Tango. They replied that they didn't have any music but not to worry as they would go off and get some. I waited on the street for them and was expecting them to come back with a portable cassette player or something. About five minutes later they came back with two men pushing a full size piano on wheels, a man with a base, a man with an accordion and a mixture of men and women of about five or six violinists!!

The orchestra played on the pavement and the two tango dancers danced in the middle of the road all for my benefit! The orchestra were superb; the dancers were superb you would have to be a very mean man to walk away from that without giving a very heavy tip. This was way before smart phones and I only had one of the very first pocket sized camcorders which was totally crap by today's standards but what I filmed that day was one of my favourite bits of amateur filming I've ever done.

Travelling around South America at that time I learnt that a lot of the older generation still resented the fact that Spain went over there and nicked all of their gold. Some of the elders feel that they are very poor today and Spain still has a lot of the wealth today that was taken from South America. So years later while I was studying advanced Spanish in Seville Spain there was a large group of us in Seville Cathedral and the guide was saying how all the lovely gold in the cathedral was traded in South America. I just couldn't resist the wind up and also I wanted to say it for the poor people in South America that had expressed their feelings to me and would never have the opportunity to go to Spain and say it.

So I said "Traded? What did they trade?" The guide said, "we traded it with coffee and tobacco". So I said, Coffee and tobacco also come from South America so you must have nicked that as well." There was a bit of an awkward silence and then the guide did the classic, "And moving on.........

It just goes to show you have to do your own research with real life and some of these guides make it all up as they go along.

Last Word

I hope you have found something from this book. This was my personal journey on the Knowledge. I have wrote about some of my background to show where my never give up attitude comes from. I went from being the weakest in life both mentally and physically to being amongst the strongest in life. I don't say this to boast as there is no glory in it for me I am anonymous writing under a nom de plume. I say this hoping to inspire anybody that feels mentally weak to know it's possible for the weakest to be amongst the strongest if they believe in themselves and face adversity and stay the course.

Never give up

Be Lucky

THIS BOOK IS AVAILABLE ON AMAZON

A. Cabman

THIS BOOK IS AVAILABLE ON AMAZON

THIS BOOK IS AVAILABLE ON AMAZON

A. Cabman

THIS BOOK IS AVAILABLE ON AMAZON

THIS BOOK IS AVAILABLE ON AMAZON

A. Cabman

Printed in Great Britain
by Amazon

41226774R00101